INTERFACES

Series Editor: Barbara Green, O.P.

Jesus Ben Sira of Jerusalem

A Biblical Guide to Living Wisely

Daniel J. Harrington, S.J.

M
G

A Michael Glazier Book

LITURGICAL PRESS

Collegeville, Minnesota

www.litpress.org

A Michael Glazier Book published by the Liturgical Press

Cover design by Ann Blattner. Watercolor by Ethel Boyle.

1	2	3	4	5	6	7	8

Library of Congress Catalog-in-Publication Data

Harrington, Daniel J.
    Jesus ben Sira of Jerusalem : a biblical guide to living wisely / Daniel J.
Harrington.
        p. cm. — (Interfaces)
    "A Michael Glazier Book."
    Summary: "Introduction to and scholarly consideration of how Jesus Ben Sira
(Jesus, the son of Sirach and Jewish wisdom teacher of the late third and early
second century B.C.E) communicated his wisdom teachings, which psychological and sociological assumptions underlay his teachings, and what they
might contribute to the personal and social formation of persons today"—Provided
by publisher.
    Includes bibliographical references and index.
    ISBN 13: 978-8146-5212-1 (pbk. : alk. paper)
    ISBN 10: 0-8146-5212-3 (pbk. : alk. paper)
    1. Bible. O.T. Apocrypha. Ecclesiasticus—Criticism, interpretation, etc. I. Title.
II. Series: Interfaces (Collegeville, Minn.)
BS1765.52.H37   2005
229'.406—dc22

                                                              2004026877

CONTENTS

PREFACE

The book you hold in your hand is one of fifteen volumes in an expanding set of volumes. This series, called INTERFACES, is a curriculum adventure, a creative opportunity in teaching and learning, presented at this moment in the long story of how the Bible has been studied, interpreted and appropriated.

The INTERFACES project was prompted by a number of experiences which you, perhaps, share. When I first taught undergraduates, the college had just received a substantial grant from the National Endowment for the Humanities, and one of the recurring courses designed within the grant was called Great Figures in Pursuit of Excellence. Three courses would be taught, each centering on a figure from some academic discipline or other, with a common seminar section to provide occasion for some integration. Some triads were more successful than others, as you might imagine. But the opportunity to concentrate on a single individual—whether historical or literary—to team teach, to make links to another pair of figures, and to learn new things about other disciplines was stimulating and fun for all involved. A second experience that gave rise to this series came at the same time, connected as well with undergraduates. It was my frequent experience to have Roman Catholic students feel quite put out about taking "more" biblical studies, since, as they confidently affirmed, they had already been there many times and done it all. That was, of course, not true; as we well know, there is always more to learn. And often those who felt most informed were the least likely to take on new information when offered it.

A stimulus as primary as my experience with students was the familiarity of listening to friends and colleagues at professional meetings talking about the research that excites us most. I often wondered: Do her undergraduate students know about this? Or how does he bring these ideas—clearly so energizing to him—into the college classroom? Perhaps some of us have felt bored with classes that seem wholly unrelated to research, that rehash the same familiar material repeatedly. Hence the idea for this series of books to bring to the fore and combine some of our research interests with our teaching and learning. Accordingly, this series is not so much about creating texts *for* student audiences but rather about *sharing* our scholarly passions with them. Because these volumes are intended each as a piece of original scholarship, they are geared to be stimulating to both students and established scholars, perhaps resulting in some fruitful collaborative learning adventures.

The series also developed from a widely shared sense that all academic fields are expanding and exploding, and that to contemplate "covering" even a testament (let alone the whole Bible or western monotheistic religions) needs to be abandoned in favor of something with greater depth and fresh focus. At the same time, the links between our fields are becoming increasingly obvious as well, and the possibilities for study which draw together academic realms that had once seemed separate is exciting. Finally, the spark of enthusiasm that almost always ignited when I mentioned to students and colleagues the idea of single figures in combination—interfacing—encouraged me that this was an idea worth trying.

And so with the leadership and help of the Liturgical Press's Academic Editor Linda Maloney, as well as with the encouragement and support of Editorial Director Mark Twomey, the series has begun to take shape.

Each volume in the INTERFACES series focuses clearly on a biblical character (or perhaps a pair of them). The characters from the first set of volumes are in some cases powerful—King Saul, Pontius Pilate—and familiar—John the Baptist, Jeremiah; in other cases they will strike you as minor and little-known—the Cannibal Mothers, Herodias. The second "litter" I added notables of various ranks and classes: Jezebel, queen of the Northern Israelite realm, James of Jerusalem and "brother of the Lord"; Simon the Pharisee, dinner host to Jesus; Legion, the Gerasene demoniac encountered so dramatically by Jesus. In this third set we find a similar contrast between apparently mighty and marginal characters: the prophet Jonah who speaks a few powerfully efficacious words; ben Sira, sage in late second temple Judah; less powerful but perhaps an even greater reading challenge stand Jephthah's daughter and Ezekiel's wife. In any case, each of them has been chosen to open up a set of worlds for consideration. The named (or unnamed) character interfaces with his or her historical-cultural world and its many issues, with other characters from biblical literature; each character has drawn forth the creativity of the author, who has taken on the challenge of engaging many readers. The books are designed for college students (though we think suitable for seminary courses and for serious Bible study), planned to provide young adults with relevant information and at a level of critical sophistication that matches the rest of the undergraduate curriculum.

In fact, the expectation is that what students are learning in other classes of historiography, literary theory, and cultural anthropology will find an echo in these books, each of which is explicit about at least two relevant methodologies. To engage at least two significant methods with some thoroughness is challenging to do. Implicit in this task is the sense that it is not possible to do all methods with depth; when several volumes of the series are used together, a balance will emerge for readers. It is surely the case that biblical studies is in a methodology-conscious moment, and the INTERFACES series embraces it enthusiastically. Our hope is for students to continue to see the relationship between their best questions and their most valuable insights, between how they approach texts and what they find there. The volumes go well beyond familiar paraphrase of narratives to ask questions that are relevant in our era. At the same time, the series authors also have each dealt with the notion of the Bible as Scripture in a way condign for them. None of the books is preachy or hortatory, and yet the self-implicating aspects of working with the revelatory text are handled frankly. The assumption is, again, that college can be a good time for people to re-examine and rethink their beliefs and assumptions, and they need to do so in good company.

The INTERFACES volumes all challenge teachers to revision radically the scope of a course, to allow the many connections among characters to serve as its warp and weft. What would emerge fresh if a Deuteronomistic History class were organized around King Saul, Queen Jezebel, and the two women who petitioned their nameless monarch? How is Jesus' ministry thrown into fresh relief when structured by shared concerns implied by a demoniac, a Pharisee, James—a disciple and John the Baptist—a mentor? And for those who must "do it all" in one semester, a study of Genesis' Joseph, Herodias and Pontius Pilate might allow for a timely foray into postcolonialism. With whom would you now place the long-suffering but doughty wife of Ezekiel: with the able Jezebel, or with the apparently-celibate Jonah? Or perhaps with Herodias? Would Jephthah's daughter organize an excellent course with the Cannibal Mothers, and perhaps as well with the Gerasene demoniac, as fresh and under-heard voices speak their words to the powerful? Would you study monarchy effectively by working with bluebloods Jezebel and Saul, as they contend with their opponents, whether those resemble John the Baptist or Pontius Pilate? Depending on the needs of your courses and students, these rich and diverse character studies will offer you many options.

The INTERFACES volumes are not substitutes for the Bible. In every case, they are to be read with the text. Quoting has been kept to a minimum, for that very reason. The series is accompanied by a straightforward companion, *From Earth's Creation to John's Revelation: The INTERFACES Biblical Storyline Companion,* which provides an overview of the whole storyline into which the characters under special study fit. The companion is available gratis for those using two or more of the INTERFACES volumes. Already readers of diverse proficiency and familiarity have registered satisfaction with this slim overview narrated by biblical Sophia.

The series challenge—for publisher, writers, teachers, and students—is to combine the volumes creatively, to INTERFACE them well so that the vast potential of the biblical text continues to unfold for us all. These ten volumes offer a foretaste of other volumes currently on the drawing board. It has been a pleasure to work with the authors of these volumes as well as with the series consultants: Carleen Mandolfo for Hebrew Bible and Catherine Murphy for New Testament. It is the hope of all of us that you will find the series useful and stimulating for your own teaching and learning.

Barbara Green, O.P.
INTERFACES Series Editor
May 16, 2005
Berkeley, California

ABBREVIATIONS

AB	Anchor Bible
BJS	Brown Judaic Studies
BZAW	Beihefte zur Zeitschrift für alttestamentliche Wissenschaft
CBQ	*Catholic Biblical Quarterly*
JSJSup	Journal for the Study of Judaism Supplements
SBLDS	Society of Biblical Literature Dissertation Series
SBLMS	Society of Biblical Literature Monograph Series
SP	Sacra Pagina
TBT	*The Bible Today*
VT	*Vetus Testamentum*
VTSup	Vetus Testamentum Supplements
WBC	Word Biblical Commentary
ZAW	*Zeitschrift für alttestamentliche Wissenschaft*

CHAPTER ONE

Ben Sira and His Book

The subject of this volume is a Jewish wisdom teacher named Jesus Ben Sira. He lived and worked in Jerusalem in the late third and early second century B.C.E. There he taught young men who wanted to become like him—a scribe, someone who not only could read and write but also was well versed in the wisdom of the ancient Near East and of the Hebrew Scriptures.

Toward the end of his career, around 180 B.C.E., Jesus Ben Sira of Jerusalem put his teachings together in a very large anthology that we call the book of Sirach (also known as Ecclesiasticus). He wrote in Hebrew. About sixty years later his grandson, living in Egypt, decided to make a Greek translation of his grandfather's book. The Greek version eventually became part of the Greek Bible and is regarded as canonical Scripture by Catholic and Orthodox Christians. While Jews and Protestants do not include Sirach in their canons of Scripture, many of them do acknowledge it as a wise and edifying book.

Wisdom books constitute a large part of the Bible. Jews and Christians alike accept Proverbs, Job, Qoheleth/Ecclesiastes, and the Song of Songs as canonical Scripture. Catholic and Orthodox Christians also include Sirach and Wisdom. Most of these books are written in the literary persona of King Solomon, the great king of ancient Israel who was famous for his wisdom, but all of them were composed many centuries after Solomon's death. The one and only ancient Jewish wisdom book that tells us its author's name and provides some personal information about him is the book of Sirach.

In a sense Jesus Ben Sira is also a literary *persona* like Solomon. Literary scholars today distinguish between the real author and the implied author of a book. For example, the real author of the novel *Moby Dick* is the nineteenth-century American writer Herman Melville. But the implied author or literary *persona* who tells the story of Captain Ahab and his quest for the great white whale "Moby Dick" is a sailor named Ishmael ("Call me Ishmael").

In the case of the book of Sirach, however, there is good reason to assume on the basis of what is said in 50:27 ("Instruction in understanding and knowledge I have written in this book, Jesus son of Eleazar son of Sirach of Jerusalem, whose mind poured forth wisdom") that the implied author and the real author are one and the same person. In that verse the author tells us his name, where he lived, and what kind of book he wrote ("instruction in understanding and knowledge"). And he claims that he is indeed the real author of this book ("whose mind poured forth wisdom"). Since the book of Sirach is the source of all we know about Jesus Ben Sira we are necessarily dealing primarily with the literary *persona* of Ben Sira. However, there is every reason to assume that behind this book there stood a Jewish wisdom teacher who flourished in what we call the early second century B.C.E.

By focusing on Jesus Ben Sira and his book this volume seeks to open up the corpus of ancient Jewish wisdom writings to beginners in biblical studies. It first provides basic information about Ben Sira and his book, as well as his world and the other biblical wisdom books. Then, on the assumption that few readers of this book have ever read and studied Sirach straight through, it provides a brief exposition of the whole book that can serve as both a guide to reading the book and a reference resource as our discussion proceeds. Then it will treat various literary, cultural-historical, and theological topics from the methodological perspectives of form criticism, social description, and biblical theology respectively. Thus it will introduce readers to how Ben Sira communicated his wise teachings, what sociological assumptions lay behind his teachings, and what these teachings might contribute to the personal and social formation of persons today.

Why are Ben Sira and his book important? Some reasons pertain to the book itself. The book of Sirach is the largest Jewish wisdom book that we have from antiquity. It is the only wisdom book that names its real author. It provides a window onto life in the land of Israel at a pivotal point in Jewish history. It illustrates how and what ancient Jewish wisdom teachers taught. And it conveys wise teachings that have challenged and inspired readers for well over two thousand years. Other reasons are extrinsic to the book. It opens up the whole corpus of biblical and extrabiblical wisdom books. It provides literary and sociocultural background to the world of Jesus and the New Testament writers. And it furnishes materials that are especially appropriate and constructive for interreligious dialogue today, since most world religions have their own rich wisdom traditions.

Jesus Ben Sira is often called a conservative and traditionalist. There is some accuracy to those descriptions, since Ben Sira was deeply rooted in the traditions of ancient Near Eastern wisdom and the Hebrew Bible, and he saw his vocation to be handing on those traditions to the next generations. However, Ben Sira's instinctive conservatism and traditionalism were balanced by his creativity and innovation in bringing together those two great traditions and integrating them into something new and different. Indeed, Ben Sira can be regarded as the first "theologian" in the Jewish and Christian traditions because he joined together secular wisdom and divine revelation (Scripture). This deeply conservative and traditional Jewish wisdom teacher laid out the path on which much greater thinkers such as Philo of Alexandria, Origen, Augustine, Thomas Aquinas, Maimonides, John Henry Newman, and Karl Rahner have traveled after him. And so we should read and study Jesus Ben Sira's book in the spirit in which he wrote it: "Observe that I have not labored for myself alone, but for all who seek wisdom" (Sir 24:34).

Ben Sira's Historical Context

Ben Sira was a wisdom teacher in Jerusalem in the late third century and early second century B.C.E.[1] If he composed his book around 180 B.C.E., that means that he was active in the middle of what is called the Second Temple period (from 538 B.C.E. to 70 C.E.)—a rather turbulent time in the land of Israel. The extent to which the teachings in the book of Sirach refer to or even allude to contemporary historical events is a matter of great debate among scholars. It is enough for our purposes to provide a brief sketch of Second Temple Jewish history as a context for an initial appreciation of the world in which Ben Sira lived and worked.

The Second Temple period in Jewish history began with the capture of Babylon by Cyrus the Great in 538 B.C.E. and his willingness to grant permission to the political and religious elite among the Jewish exile community there to return to Jerusalem (see Isaiah 40–55). The rebuilding of Jerusalem and its Temple as well as the restoration of the Jewish community in the late sixth century B.C.E. was a slow and often disappointing process (see Haggai, Zechariah, and Isaiah 56–66). Nevertheless, under Ezra and Nehemiah the Judeans were able to work out a politically viable relationship with the rulers of the Persian empire and to enjoy some measure of social stability and religious identity during the fifth century.

---

[1] Martin Hengel, *Judaism and Hellenism* (Philadelphia: Fortress, 1974).

In the mid-fourth century B.C.E. Alexander the Great's conquest of Egypt and the Persian empire brought a change of rulers to the land of Israel. When Alexander died in 323 B.C.E. there was a great struggle for power among his generals and friends, and eventually his vast empire was divided into parts. By around the year 300 the people of Judea found themselves basically under the rule of the Ptolemies, the Hellenistic dynasty whose base was in Egypt. The Ptolemaic imperial policy was relatively "hands-off" as long as taxes were paid to them, and so the Judeans enjoyed some measure of autonomy.

Nevertheless, during the third century there was a constant struggle between the Ptolemies to the south and the powerful Seleucid dynasty to the north in Syria. Of course Israel found itself geographically in the middle of this struggle. Finally in 200 B.C.E. the Seleucid king Antiochus III defeated the Ptolemies and brought the Jews of Palestine into his Seleucid empire. His successor Seleucus IV (187–175 B.C.E.) was eventually replaced by Antiochus IV Epiphanes (175–163). Then the intrusive policies of Antiochus IV brought political and religious repression upon the Jews of Jerusalem and issued in the revolt led by the Jewish Maccabee family in 164 B.C.E. (see Daniel, and 1 and 2 Maccabees).

If he wrote his book around 180 B.C.E., Ben Sira of Jerusalem would certainly have experienced the transition from Ptolemaic to Seleucid rule around 200 B.C.E. and the turmoil associated with it. But he had probably died before matters became even more tumultuous with Antiochus IV and his Jewish collaborators' efforts at turning Jerusalem into a Greek city *(polis)*. Yet he may well have witnessed the ouster of the legitimate high priest Onias III in 175, when his brother Jason promised Antiochus more revenues, and then Jason's own removal in 172 when Jason was in turn outbid by a certain Menelaus for the high priesthood. Note the Greek names "Jason" and "Menelaus," which suggest that a cultural and religious shift from traditional Judaism to Hellenism was under way in these developments. Ben Sira was a great supporter of the Jerusalem Temple and the priesthood, and was conservative and traditional by nature. These events must have been greatly disturbing to him, though he makes no obvious direct comments on them in his book (thus suggesting that it was already written before these events took place).

Ben Sira and His Book

As we have said, the author of the book of Sirach was a Jewish wisdom teacher active in Jerusalem in the early second century B.C.E. Near the end of his book according to the Greek version the author identifies himself by name: "Jesus son of Eleazar son of Sirach of Jerusalem" (50:27). The author's own name was "Jesus," a form of Joshua ("the Lord saves") that was fairly common around the time of Jesus of Nazareth. Eleazar was his father's name, and Sira was the name of his grandfather. Sirach is the Greek form of the Hebrew name Sira (with the final -*ch* representing the final Hebrew letter aleph or simply designating the name as indeclinable in Greek).[2]

The title given to this book in most Greek manuscripts is "Wisdom of Jesus the Son of Sirach." Latin manuscripts refer to it as the "Book of Jesus the Son of Sirach." In the Latin tradition the book is customarily called "Ecclesiasticus," which means "church book," probably a statement about its acceptance into the Christian canon of Scripture. The Hebrew manuscripts give no firm indication of the book's original title, but (if there was one at all) it was probably something like "Wisdom of Jesus the Son of Sira." Most scholars today refer to the book as "Sirach" and to its author as "Ben Sira." They use the Hebrew word for "son" *(ben)* and the grandfather's name because Jesus and Eleazar were common names while "Sira" was quite rare and therefore is distinctive. Some scholars use the title "Sirach" to refer to the Greek version, "Ecclesiasticus" to refer to the Latin version, and "Ben Sira" to speak about the Hebrew manuscripts or the original Hebrew text. In this book I use "Sirach" generally to designate the book, and "Ben Sira" to designate the author.

What can be said about Ben Sira the author must be deduced from material in his book. There are no independent sources of information about him from antiquity. In what is presented as an autobiographical poem at the very end of the book (51:13-30) Ben Sira describes his personal search for wisdom (51:13-22) and issues an invitation to study at his wisdom school (51:23-30).

Ben Sira's quest for wisdom began in the prayer of petition ("I sought wisdom openly in my prayer," 51:13) and in connection with worship at the Jerusalem Temple. He makes no sharp distinction between the search for wisdom and the temple cult. In fact, his school may well have been associated with the Jerusalem Temple. He recognized that gaining real wisdom also involved the hard work of study ("I found for myself much instruction," 51:16) and living in an appropriate manner ("in my conduct I was strict," 51:19). However, in his mind the quest was well worth the effort, since he eventually found delight in wisdom ("my heart delighted in her," 51:15) and looked upon wisdom as his "prize possession" (51:21). As Ben Sira's search begins in the prayer of petition for the gift of wisdom, so

[2] For this interpretation see Patrick W. Skehan and Alexander A. Di Lella, *The Wisdom of Ben Sira.* AB 39 (Garden City, NY: Doubleday, 1987) 3.

it ends in the prayer of thanksgiving for the gift he received: "The Lord gave me my tongue as a reward, and I will praise him with it" (51:22).

The second part of the autobiographical poem (51:23-30) is an kind of advertisement or "info-mercial" for Ben Sira's wisdom school. He begins by issuing an invitation to the "uneducated" to "lodge in my house of instruction" (51:23). From the bulk of Ben Sira's book we can deduce that the curriculum combined traditional wisdom teachings (proverbs, parables, etc.) and biblical studies (the revealed wisdom of the Hebrew Scriptures). While there seems to have been no set tuition ("acquire wisdom for yourselves without money," 51:25), we can presume that donations were accepted or that there was some other source of financial support. At any rate, Ben Sira promises prospective students rewards of "silver and gold" (51:28). He uses the image of the "yoke" (a harness placed on beasts of burden as they pulled a plow or powered a mill) for the hard work expected from his students, and offers "much serenity" in return. See Jesus of Nazareth's use of the same images in Matt 11:28-29: "Take my yoke upon you . . . and you will find rest for your souls." Ever the schoolmaster, Ben Sira insists in closing that his students must complete their assignments on time: "Do your work in good time, and in his own time God will give you your reward" (51:30).

At various points in his book Ben Sira uses first person singular ("I") language to describe the quest for wisdom and the role of the wisdom teacher. In 33:16-19 he compares himself to a gleaner who follows the grape pickers in the hope of getting what they might miss and leave behind. Thus he acknowledges his place at the end of a long tradition of wisdom seekers and teachers, and he thanks God for allowing him to fill his own winepress with grapes. In 34:9-12 he notes that his search for wisdom has involved travel ("I have seen many things in my travels," 34:12) and acknowledges that he was often in danger of death because of these journeys.

As a teacher of wisdom Ben Sira in 24:30-34 compares himself to a tributary or small stream coming off from a mighty river: "As for me, I was like a canal from a river, like a water channel into a garden" (24:30). Thus he modestly admits the derivative character of his teaching, and indeed glories in his role as a vehicle for handing on the great wisdom tradition. He claims that he has labored "not for myself alone, but for all who seek wisdom" (24:34).

In introducing his poem on "all the works of the Lord" in 39:12-35, Ben Sira compares himself to the "full moon" (39:12), bursting with knowledge and wonder at what God has created. He goes on to describe his audience as being "like a rose growing by a stream of water" (39:13), thus evoking again the images of himself as a canal or water channel for the great river of wisdom.

Ben Sira presided over a wisdom school (a "house of instruction") in Jerusalem in the early second century B.C.E. He arrived at his position through divine enlightenment and disciplined study. He had searched for wisdom and found it, and so he invited younger people to join him in that search. He loved his work as a Jewish wisdom teacher and regarded it as important for himself and for the good of society in general.

The work known as the "Wisdom of Ben Sira" is generally classified as a "wisdom book." It assumes a situation in which Ben Sira, an experienced sage, is instructing younger persons who wish to become wise. The prospective students are males, persons who have the financial resources and leisure for study, and who will themselves become sages, heads of households, and leaders among their Jewish contemporaries. They are being trained to serve as "scribes"—not simply those who can read and write competently, but also and especially those who are preparing to exercise public leadership (see 38:24–39:11). At his school in Jerusalem, Ben Sira specialized in showing his students how to join together ancient Near Eastern wisdom traditions and the distinctively Jewish religious traditions embodied in the Hebrew Scriptures.

Ben Sira's basic and most important theological insight is that the highest form of wisdom is to be found in the Torah (the first five books of the Hebrew Bible) and that the proper response to the gift of wisdom is "fear of the Lord." His theological genius was to integrate the secular wisdom tradition based on human experience and practical insight with the particular revelation of the God of Israel in nature, the Torah, and history.

As a wisdom teacher Ben Sira generally follows the literary conventions of Jewish and ancient Near Eastern wisdom teachers. His basic method of communication is through short sayings of two members in synonymous (similar ideas) or antithetical (opposite ideas) parallelism. He often joins individual sayings on related topics to develop a theme or even an argument in the form of a paragraph. He especially values the "instruction" form in which he presents advice on various topics to "my son" or "my children." See Chapter Four for an extended discussion of the literary forms used by Ben Sira to convey his sage advice.

His Grandson's Greek Translation

Although Ben Sira wrote his book in Hebrew and we now again have access to parts of his Hebrew text, the most complete and influential version of his book is the Greek translation made by his grandson in Egypt in the late second century B.C.E. The "prologue" printed in our Bibles as a preface to Ben Sira's book provides important information about the book and about the process of its transmission. The prologue consists of three long sentences, each now forming a single paragraph, written in relatively elegant and sophisticated Greek. It offers insights into the nature of the book, the problem of translating it, and the process of the translation.

The writer of the prologue speaks about "my grandfather Jesus," and so the Greek translator identifies himself as the author's grandson. The grandson says that he came from Israel to Egypt in the thirty-eighth year (132 B.C.E.) of the reign of Ptolemy VIII Euergetes II, and seems to have completed his work of translation around the time of that Egyptian ruler's death (117 B.C.E.). There was a large Jewish community in Egypt in the second century B.C.E., and this seems to have been the main audience intended for the Greek version.

Ben Sira's grandson does not characterize the work simply as a wisdom book. He is well aware of his grandfather's dedication to the Hebrew Scriptures ("the Law and the Prophets and the others") and of his project of bringing them into harmony with the best insights of the ancient Near Eastern wisdom tradition so that Jews might make "even greater progress in living according to the law." From his prologue we are told at the outset that Ben Sira presents his wise teachings in the context of divine revelation (the Hebrew Scriptures) and hopes to help his fellow Jews become better and wiser Jews.

The grandson's translation was a labor of love. The "love" part arose from his conviction that his grandfather had much to say to the many Jews outside the land of Israel who were not fluent in Hebrew. By translating the book into Greek, the grandson sought to make it available to Jews and even "outsiders" in Egypt and all over the Greco-Roman world. The "labor" part is clear from the grandson's comment about how "I have applied my skill day and night to complete and publish the book." He does not appear to have been a veteran or "professional" translator, but instead someone who took up his task out of family piety and belief in the abiding value of his grandfather's book.

Nevertheless, the grandson was aware of the difficulties and deficiencies involved in his translation. He knew the truth of the Italian proverb *tradutorre traditore* ("a translator is a traitor"). Besides apologizing for having perhaps "rendered some phrases imperfectly," he notes that "what was originally expressed in Hebrew does not have exactly the same sense when translated into another language." He observes that in general the Greek translations of what we call the Hebrew Bible "differ not a little" when read against the Hebrew originals.[3] Nevertheless, rather than making

---

[3] Ben G. Wright, *No Small Difference: Sirach's Relationship to its Hebrew Parent Text.* Society of Biblical Literature Septuagint and Cognate Studies 26 (Atlanta: Scholars, 1989).

his translation in the elegant and sophisticated Greek (paraphrase) of which he shows himself capable in his prologue, the grandson chose to follow the translation philosophy of "formal equivalence" (literal translation of the Hebrew) which is generally at work in the Greek translations of the Hebrew Bible in the Septuagint. In other words, he generally let the Semitic vocabulary and syntax of his grandfather's book show through in the translation while adapting the Hebrew text to the rules and limitations of the Greek language.

Texts and Translations of the Book

The Greek translation of Sirach prepared by the author's grandson became the primary (canonical) text among Christians and the source of the Latin and most other early versions. Sirach was not admitted to the more restricted Jewish canon of Hebrew Scriptures that emerged in the late first century C.E., probably because it was composed "too late" in comparison with the other books. But it was transmitted as part of the larger Greek collection of Jewish sacred writings known as the Septuagint.[4] The Christian churches generally followed the wider Greek Septuagint canon, and for fifteen centuries almost all Christians regarded Sirach as "Sacred Scripture."

When Martin Luther and other early Protestant Reformers (following a suggestion by Jerome) decided in the sixteenth century to limit their Old Testament canon to the Jewish Hebrew canon, Sirach and other books among the so-called Apocrypha were at best relegated to a secondary status as "deuterocanonical" books and were printed in a separate section between the Old and New Testaments. The Roman Catholic and Orthodox Christian churches continued to include Sirach in their canons.

While Jews never considered Sirach to be canonical Sacred Scripture, they continued to respect and quote the book, often in its Hebrew form. As a result, the Hebrew text was not entirely lost after the Greek translation. It continued to be used at Qumran and Masada where the earliest fragments were found, served as the basis for the Syriac version, and was copied at least up to the eleventh and twelfth centuries. However, the Hebrew form of the book of Sirach became increasingly marginalized among Jews, perhaps in reaction to the book's extensive use by Christians in the patristic and medieval periods. Christians used the Greek and Latin versions as their canonical texts, and so the Hebrew original became effectively lost for several centuries.

---

[4] For information about these books and their significance see Daniel J. Harrington, *Invitation to the Apocrypha* (Grand Rapids: Eerdmans, 1999).

In 1896 and thereafter, substantial parts of the Hebrew text of Sirach were recovered from the Cairo Genizah, a kind of storeroom for old manuscripts in a Jewish synagogue in Cairo, Egypt. These Hebrew texts are regarded by scholars as generally authentic representatives of Ben Sira's Hebrew original, though there is some evidence of retranslation from the Syriac version. In 1964 several chapters of the Hebrew text were found at Masada, the famous outpost in Israel where Jewish rebels made their last stand against the Roman army in 74 B.C.E.[5]

Even in antiquity both the Greek and the Hebrew textual traditions had short and long editions or recensions. And so the book of Sirach presents many fascinating philological problems for textual critics seeking to determine the earliest Hebrew or Greek text and for translators who are challenged to find the best basis on which to produce their translations into modern languages. To cite one very important example, it appears that all the Greek manuscripts contain a textual displacement by which Sirach 30:25–33:13a and 33:13b–36:16a have changed places.

Much of the best technical scholarship on Sirach has necessarily focused on establishing the best text, explaining the relationships between the Hebrew and Greek versions, and producing the best translations.[6] Most modern translators use the Greek version as their basic text, since it is the most complete version and has served as the "church's book" ("Ecclesiasticus") throughout the centuries. They follow the text and numbering system in the exemplary critical edition of the Greek text prepared by Joseph Ziegler and published in 1965.[7] They may, however, call upon readings in the Hebrew manuscripts to correct mistakes or corruptions in the Greek textual tradition or to represent more accurately what they judge Ben Sira wanted to say. Some translations distinguish the short (and generally better) and the long Greek recensions or editions by using different typefaces or by relegating the additional sayings to the foot of the pages.

The focus of this book, however, is not textual criticism or philology. Rather, its focus is Ben Sira, the second century B.C.E. Jewish wisdom teacher based in Jerusalem, and the literary artistry, historical and cultural assumptions, and theological significance of his book. In other words, our principal concerns are the author of the book of Sirach and how he commu-

---

[5] All the Hebrew texts are collected by Pancratius C. Beentjes in *The Book of Ben Sira. Vetus Testamentum Supplements* 68 (Leiden: Brill, 1997).

[6] See Pancratius C. Beentjes, ed., *The Book of Sirach in Modern Research.* BZAW 255 (Berlin and New York: de Gruyter, 1997); and Richard J. Coggins, *Sirach* (Sheffield: Sheffield Academic Press, 1998).

[7] Joseph Ziegler, ed., *Sapientia Iesu Filii Sirach.* Septuaginta 12/2 (Göttingen: Vandenhoeck & Ruprecht, 1965).

nicated his message, what he took over from the world and culture in which he wrote, and what he had to say in comparison with other Jewish wisdom teachers in antiquity and what he may say to seekers of wisdom today.

Instead of involving the nonspecialist audience for whom this book is intended in specialized textual and linguistic problems, I have generally followed the English text according to the New Revised Standard Version (1989). This translation embodies modern scholarship, uses current (and inclusive) English, and is readily available in the U.S. and many other parts of the world. It should be noted, however, that the NRSV's generally laudable policy of using gender-inclusive language with reference to humans occasionally distorts Ben Sira's (and his grandson's) male-oriented and patriarchal language. Where there is danger of a serious misunderstanding of Ben Sira's point, I will make note of it.

Conclusion

This chapter has provided a brief introduction to Jesus Ben Sira, a Jewish wisdom teacher in Jerusalem. Although he lived through turbulent times, he tried to impart a wisdom that transcended the particular circumstances of his own situation. Around 180 B.C.E. he wrote a very large book in Hebrew "for all who seek wisdom" (24:34). His book was lovingly translated into Greek by his grandson in Egypt around 117 B.C.E. Eventually this book became part of the Christian canon of Sacred Scripture and has remained such in the Catholic and Orthodox churches. It is also read and respected by Jews and Protestant Christians, though they do not regard it as Sacred Scripture. Ben Sira's goal in writing his book for all who seek wisdom has been fulfilled probably beyond its author's wildest dreams. Not many books are still read over two thousand years after their composition! The goal of this book is to introduce Ben Sira and his book to a new generation of readers. The following chapters will work toward that goal.

CHAPTER TWO

Ben Sira and Other Wisdom Books

Ben Sira did not write his book in an intellectual and spiritual vacuum.[1] Rather, he was part of a movement that reaches back to some of the earliest documents we have from the ancient Near East and has several representatives among the books of the Bible. He had many predecessors and successors. Almost all these texts take as their implied author some great figure of the distant past (Solomon) or the recent past (Jesus, James). The book of Sirach is noteworthy because in this case the implied author and the real author seem to be one and the same person.

The most extensive and representative wisdom writing in the Hebrew Bible is the book of Proverbs. It is in fact an anthology of smaller wisdom collections taking the form of instructions about wisdom (chs. 1–9) and examples of wisdom generally expressed in short sayings ("proverbs") that encapsulate practical wisdom based on experience and intended to guide one through the everyday (chs. 10–31).

The books of Qoheleth/Ecclesiastes and Job take issue with the "law of retribution," which is basic to the outlook of Proverbs and of the ancient wisdom movement in general. According to the law of retribution wise and righteous persons are rewarded in this life, while foolish and unrighteous persons are punished. Qoheleth/Ecclesiastes often casts doubt on the adequacy of the law of retribution to explain actual human experience. Job is a

---

[1] For general introductions to the wisdom writings see Richard J. Clifford, *The Wisdom Literature* (Nashville: Abingdon, 1998); James L. Crenshaw, *Old Testament Wisdom: An Introduction* (Louisville: Westminster John Knox, 1998); and Roland E. Murphy, *The Tree of Life* (rev. ed. Grand Rapids: Eerdmans, 2002). See also John J. Collins, *Jewish Wisdom in the Hellenistic Age* (Louisville: John Knox, 1997).

relentless exploration of the problem posed by innocent suffering with regard to the alleged omnipotence and justice of God.

These biblical wisdom books constitute part of the Jewish contribution to the international wisdom movement well represented in ancient literature from Mesopotamia and Egypt. The Jewish authors struggled to
integrate the secular perspectives of the international wisdom movement
into their distinctive theological framework and their relatively clear ideas
about God. The Jewish wisdom writers took King Solomon as their exemplar and "patron saint." According to 1 Kings 4:29-34 God gave Solomon
"very great wisdom, discernment, and breadth of understanding . . . so that
Solomon's wisdom surpassed the wisdom of all the people of the east."

The three wisdom books of the Hebrew Bible were put in their present
literary forms in early postexilic times, from the 6th to the 3rd centuries B.C.E.,
though some (especially Proverbs) may incorporate older material. There is
debate about the settings in which these wisdom teachings were developed,
formulated, and handed on. Was it the royal court, or the school, or the
family/clan? Or was it a combination of all three settings to some extent?

Those who follow the wider canon of Scripture (as Catholic and Orthodox Christians do) regard two other wisdom books—Sirach and Wisdom
—as Sacred Scripture. As we have seen and will see, the book of Sirach is
very successful in integrating the concerns of "secular" wisdom (about social relations, family obligations, money, happiness, etc.) into the framework of biblical Judaism. Wisdom (written at Alexandria in the 1st century
B.C.E.) is more a book *about* wisdom rather than a book *of* wisdom. It chiefly
concerns the nature of wisdom and wisdom's role in biblical history and
life today instead of giving practical advice about living wisely.

Since these books will be major sources in our "Interfaces" with the
book of Sirach in Chapter 6 and elsewhere in the book, it is important at this
point to provide some basic information about them as well as a major wisdom book among the Dead Sea scrolls (4QInstruction) and two New Testament wisdom instructions (the Sermon on the Mount and the letter of James).

Proverbs

The book of Proverbs is in fact a collection of several smaller wisdom
texts.[2] The whole collection is placed under the patronage of Solomon in
the opening verse: "The proverbs of Solomon son of David, king of Israel"

[2] See Raymond Van Leeuwen, "Proverbs," in *New Interpreter's Bible* (Nashville: Abingdon, 1997) 5:17–264; Roland E. Murphy, *Proverbs*. WBC 18A (Waco: Word Books, 1998);
Richard J. Clifford, *Proverbs*. Old Testament Library (Louisville: Westminster John Knox,
1999); and Michael V. Fox, *Proverbs 1–9*, AB 19A (New York: Doubleday, 2000).

(1:1). The Wisdom Poems in chapters 1–9 provide the theological lenses through which readers are expected to view the practical advice given in the remaining sections. The heart of this book is the large anthology of individual proverbs or maxims in the Proverbs of Solomon (10:1–22:16), which may well be the oldest (pre-exilic?) part of the present book. Then there are Admonitions (22:17–24:22), the Sayings of the Wise (24:23-34), the Proverbs of Solomon (25:1–29:27), the Words of Agur (30:1-33), the Words of Lemuel's Mother (31:1-9), and the poem about the Ideal Wife (31:10-31).

The Wisdom Poems in the first nine chapters are generally regarded as from the early post-exilic period: that is, from the 6th to the 4th centuries B.C.E. They offer readers the key concepts that can help them make sense of and assimilate the many wise teachings that follow. These poems describe the goodness of wisdom as something more precious than any other possession, and as bringing great rewards. They draw sharp contrasts between the wise and the foolish, between the righteous and the wicked. They also develop and contrast the figures of Lady Wisdom and Dame Folly (or the Foreign Woman), who lead persons either to wisdom and happiness (Lady Wisdom) or to folly and perdition (Dame Folly) respectively. These poems also integrate the standard secular wisdom vocabulary and concerns with the traditional Jewish religious vocabulary: "The fear of the Lord is the beginning of knowledge" (1:7). And they repeat many times over the law of retribution according to which wise and righteous behavior leads to happiness and a long life while foolish and wicked behavior results in calamity and death.

The Proverbs of Solomon in 10:1–22:16 is an anthology of some 375 sayings on various topics. There is no systematic arrangement of the sayings, though there are some blocks on similar topics. The proverbs generally convey secular wisdom with only occasional mentions of the God of Israel. The sayings are based on personal or communal experiences or observations and often communicate through comparisons taken from everyday life: "Like vinegar to the teeth, and smoke to the eyes, so are the lazy to their employers" (10:26). The sayings are not scientific laws, which are presumably always and everywhere accurate. But they are supposed to hold true in the vast majority of cases.

The Admonitions in Proverbs 22:17–24:22 are generally regarded by scholars as dependent in some way on the much earlier Egyptian "Instruction of Amen-em-opet." The parallels are so many and striking that it appears that the biblical writer had access to something like the Egyptian text as a source. For example, the second "chapter" in "Amen-em-opet" warns against robbing the oppressed and being overbearing toward the disabled. This advice is echoed in Prov 22:22: "Do not rob the poor because they are poor, or crush the afflicted at the gate." What makes the biblical version of this admonition distinctive is the theological motivation supplied in Prov 22:23: "for the Lord pleads their cause and despoils of life those who despoil them." This example illustrates both the international character of the wisdom movement in antiquity and the distinctive religious insights that Jewish wisdom teachers brought to it. The biblical conviction that God hears the cries of the poor and takes their side adds a new dimension to the secular wisdom tradition.

Proverbs ends in 31:10-31 with the Poem about the Ideal Wife. This poem was probably an originally independent piece added to the anthology as a kind of "bookend" to the portrayals of Lady Wisdom and Dame Folly in the first nine chapters. It is an acrostic, with each line beginning with a new letter in the Hebrew alphabet (*aleph, beth, gimel,* and so on). It shares the assumptions of a patriarchal society regarding the subordinate place of women, and presupposes a large (and wealthy) household that is overseen by a very capable woman. The poem begins by reflecting on what a great help to her husband this capable woman is (31:10-12), and then describes in detail the activities of the good wife while she runs the household as an effective manager (31:13-20). She even sees to the needs of all her household members (including servants and slaves), and so is rightly praised by all in her society (31:21-29). The conclusion to the poem (31:30-31) describes this ideal wife-mother-manager as one who "fears the Lord." Indeed, the real source of all her virtues and managerial skills is precisely her fear of the Lord. While assuming an androcentric vision of society, this poem describes what passed for the ideal of womanhood in ancient Near Eastern societies, especially among its elite members.

It is likely that Ben Sira knew and used the book of Proverbs as a source in his teaching and writing. He employed its primary modes of communication (maxims or proverbs, instructions, etc.), shared its cultural assumptions (about honor and shame, about women, etc.), and developed many of its theological insights (the value of seeking wisdom, fear of the Lord, etc.). What makes Ben Sira's book stand out from Proverbs is his more sweeping program of integrating the secular wisdom traditions of the ancient Near East with Israel's distinctive religious traditions.

Job

The book of Job is one of the greatest books in the Bible and indeed in world literature.[3] While it is generally classified as a wisdom book with

[3] See Norman Habel, *The Book of Job.* Old Testament Library (Philadelphia: Westminster, 1985); Gustavo Gutiérrez, *On Job: God-Talk and the Suffering of the Innocent* (Maryknoll,

Proverbs, Qoheleth/Ecclesiastes, and Sirach, it does not offer much by way of proverbs or wisdom instructions. Rather, it is a relentlessly critical exploration of a central tenet of the Jewish and international wisdom movement: the law of retribution. According to that principle wise and righteous persons are rewarded in this life, and foolish and wicked persons eventually suffer and die.

The book of Job deals with the case of Job, who is the exemplar of wisdom and righteousness: "that man was blameless and upright, one who feared God, and turned away from evil" (1:1). According to the prologue of the book (chs. 1–2) God allows Satan to put Job to two tests, one involving his possessions and family and the other involving his own physical health. While Job apparently emerges from these tests as the model of resignation and patience (see 1:21; 2:10), in chapter 3 we meet a very different Job, one who laments his present condition, curses the day of his birth and the night of his conception, and looks forward to his death as bringing rest and release from suffering.

The suffering of the wise and righteous Job calls into question a basic axiom of the wisdom movement: that wise and righteous persons always prosper. His three friends arrive (2:11-13) to offer sympathy and consolation. However, once Job begins to complain about his situation and to raise questions about it they feel compelled to enter into debate with him. The subject of their debate is what is often called theodicy; that is, the effort to explain, justify *(dikaioō),* and defend the ways of God *(theos).* The effort at theodicy seeks to hold together three propositions: God is all powerful; God is just; and innocent persons suffer. The question is: How can an omnipotent and just God allow wise and righteous persons to suffer?

The main part of the book of Job consists of three cycles of three debates between Job and his three friends, along with a final intervention by Elihu (chs. 32–37). In these debates the friends imagine they are defending God's omnipotence and justice, and they contend that Job must have sinned precisely because he is suffering, and urge him to confess his sins. For his part Job insists that he has not sinned, and he calls into question the proposition that God is just. The debates end in a stalemate, until God in chapters 38–41 speaks from the whirlwind and advises Job to turn away from his narrow and self-centered viewpoint and to try to look at the world from God's perspective. In chapter 42 Job relents and appears to embrace God's

---

NY: Orbis, 1987); and Carol Newsom, "Job," in *New Interpreter's Bible* (Nashville: Abingdon, 1997) 4:317–637.

solution. Then his possessions, family, and health are restored in greater abundance. At this point God rejects the position of Job's friends: "for you have not spoken of me what is right, as my servant Job has" (42:7).

The book of Job is set long ago and far away "in the land of Uz" (1:1). It makes no mention of Moses and the Law revealed on Mount Sinai. It is even not at all clear that we are to assume that Job is Jewish. While most interpreters place the book's actual composition against the background of the exile and return (6th to 4th centuries B.C.E.), there is no explicit reference to these events or to any other events in ancient Israel's history. Many scholars suppose that the prologue (chs. 1–2) and the epilogue (ch. 42) constituted an earlier prose narrative (supporting the law of retribution) into which the poetic debates and speeches (questioning the law of retribution) have been inserted. But the debates and speeches are what make the book of Job so important, because they represent an extensive and fearless critical investigation of the truth of the law of retribution (that people get what they deserve in this life). The wisdom movement provides the background for the exploration, and the book of Job takes a critical stance toward it.

The poetic interlude in Job 28 about how hard it is for humans to find wisdom is especially relevant for the book's theme. The poem first (28:1-11) describes the remarkable ingenuity and skill that humans show in finding gold and precious stones. Then it raises the real question of the poem and of the entire book: "But where shall wisdom be found? And where is the place of understanding?" (28:12). The poem goes on (28:13-22) to deny that humans know the way to wisdom and where it is to be found. It insists that only God understands the way to wisdom and its place (28:23-27), and so the search for wisdom (and for the definitive solution to the problem of innocent suffering) is beyond unaided human capacity. The poem concludes by observing that the best that humans can do for now is to fear the Lord and depart from evil (28:28). While criticizing one basic principle of the wisdom movement (the law of retribution), the book of Job nonetheless confirms as foundational two other principles of the Jewish wisdom movement: fear of the Lord and righteous conduct.

In his catalogue of biblical heroes in chapters 44–50 Ben Sira did not include Job's complaints. While in 49:9 he applauded the figure of Job in the prose narrative (chs. 1–2 and 42), he would have objected to much of what is said in the heart of the book, especially by Job. Ben Sira was more confident about the possibility of attaining wisdom in this life and more credulous regarding the law of retribution. Indeed, one of the deficiencies of Ben Sira's book is his failure to face the problem of innocent suffering. His attempt through the doctrine of the "pairs" seems feeble in comparison with the fearless exploration presented in the book of Job.

Qoheleth/Ecclesiastes

An even more critical treatment of some assumptions of the wisdom movement appears in the book known as Qoheleth in its Hebrew version and Ecclesiastes in its Greek version.[4] The word "Qoheleth" derives from the Hebrew verb "gather" *(qāhal),* and is traditionally rendered as "Preacher" or "Teacher." The Greek equivalent is "Ecclesiastes" (like the Greek word *ekklēsia* for church). Early on in this book there is some effort to associate its author with Solomon, the patron of the Jewish wisdom movement. In 1:1 Qoheleth is described as "son of David, king in Jerusalem," and in 1:12 the implied author refers to himself as "king over Israel in Jerusalem." In 2:1-11 he recounts his exploits and describes his possessions in terms reminiscent of the description of Solomon in 1 Kings. But then the device of identifying Qoheleth and Solomon fades away, and the book presents itself as what it really is: the memoirs of an outspoken and unusual Jewish wisdom teacher.

The book of Qoheleth is generally attributed to a wisdom teacher active in Jerusalem in the 3rd century B.C.E. It covers many topics in no obvious logical order. What makes this anthology distinctive is its experiential methodology and its critical outlook on standard topics treated by wisdom teachers. The author has been variously called a skeptic, a pessimist, a depressive, and an existentialist. He regards human striving after wisdom and happiness as futile, the law of retribution as inadequate and not justified by experience, and death as the great equalizer casting its shadow over all human endeavors. The presence of this book in the Jewish and Christian canons of Sacred Scripture provides an example of critical thinking within the biblical tradition, and there are times in our lives when its negativity offers consolation and even (ironically) hope.

According to Qoheleth, human striving after the most noble goals is doomed to fail. In 1:1-11 he reflects on the futility of all earthly things and declares that striving after them is *hebel* ("breath, wind, emptiness, vanity"). Even searching for wisdom and knowledge turns out to be "a chasing after wind" (1:12-18). Adopting the *persona* of Solomon, the author in 2:1-11 claims to have tested the values of pleasure derived from laughter, wine, grand building projects, slaves, possessions of all sorts, money, entertainments, and concubines. His experiments led him to conclude that "all was vanity and chasing after wind."

[4] See Roland E. Murphy, *Ecclesiastes.* WBC 23 (Dallas: Word Books, 1992); Choon-Leong Seow, *Ecclesiastes.* AB 18C (New York: Doubleday, 1997); and W. Sibley Towner, "Ecclesiastes," in *New Interpreter's Bible* (Nashville: Abingdon, 1997) 5:265–360.

Neither wisdom (2:12-17) nor hard work (2:18-26) brings real happiness. In the end the search for wisdom itself is futile, the wise and foolish alike die, and both are soon forgotten. Likewise, the fruits of all one's hard work may well end up as the property of foolish children who will squander all the results of one's hard work. While there is "a time for every matter under heaven: a time to be born, and a time to die . . ." (3:1-2), the problem is knowing exactly when that time comes, since "they (humans) cannot find out what God has done from the beginning to the end" (3:11).

For Qoheleth the law of retribution (the wise and righteous are rewarded, and the foolish and wicked are punished) is not verified by human experience. In 3:17 he floats the idea that "God will judge the righteous and the wicked." But Qoheleth is not at all sure that there is any life after death for humans. He is by no means certain that "the human spirit goes upward" (3:21), and he goes on to declare that the dead are more fortunate than the living, and that better than both is "the one who has not yet been" (4:3). From 4:7 onward Qoheleth treats from his characteristic critical perspective some common wisdom topics such as friendship, speech, rich and poor, women, and so forth. In 7:15-18 he takes direct aim at the law of retribution, and recounts the results of his experiences: "there are righteous people who perish in their righteousness, and there are wicked people who prolong their life in their evil doing" (7:15).

The idea of death as the great equalizer runs through the entire book but increases in importance as it moves toward its ending. According to Qoheleth the law of retribution does not apply in the present life (see 7:15), and there is no reason to think that all will be made right in some form of life after death. The same fate—death—comes to all humans, whether they are righteous or wicked, wise or foolish (9:2, 3). And in what is perhaps the most pessimistic statement in the book Qoheleth concludes that "the dead know nothing; they have no more reward, and even the memory of them is lost" (9:5).

Qoheleth's recipe for happiness, however limited it may be, is to live life in moderation and enjoy the simple pleasures that come your way. For him God seems distant and even uninvolved in human existence, and it is nearly impossible for humans to understand the ways of God with the world. In the meantime young people are advised to "follow the inclination of your heart and the desire of your eyes" (11:9).

The point of Qoheleth's marvelous picture of the aging process in 12:1-8 is to remind his readers to enjoy life in the present, while they still can. Out of all his searches for wisdom and pleasure Qoheleth has come to the conclusion that a little happiness can be found among all the toil and emptiness of human existence. He explains the human condition in these terms: "This is what I have seen to be good: it is fitting to eat and drink and find enjoyment in all the toil with which one toils under the sun the few days of the life that God gives us; for this is our lot" (5:18).

The books of Sirach and Qoheleth are alike insofar as they give the impression that a real individual is behind each of them. But how different they are! In fact, it is possible that Ben Sira wrote explicitly to counter the pessimism of Qoheleth and refute his skepticism. If Qoheleth sees the glass as almost empty, Ben Sira views it as almost full. Ben Sira is very optimistic about discerning the presence of God, the value of seeking and finding wisdom, and the possibility of attaining happiness by living according to wisdom teachings. Both writers are vague about life after death. However, Ben Sira is more positive about life here and now, perhaps because he avoids the challenges Qoheleth raises about the doctrine of retribution and the problem of innocent suffering.

4QInstruction: A Wisdom Text from Qumran

The text known as 4QInstruction (a wisdom instruction found in Cave 4 at Qumran and formerly known as Sapiential Work A) is the most extensive example of a wisdom instruction among the Dead Sea scrolls.[5] Until its recovery in the early 1950s this work was unknown for almost two thousand years. It appears in at least six fragmentary manuscripts and so ranks among the best represented works found at Qumran. The beginning of the text (4Q416 1) sets everything that follows in a cosmic ("the host of heaven He has established") and eschatological ("all iniquity shall come to an end until the epoch of destruction will be finished") framework. Indeed, the most important and distinctive feature of the book is its integration of creation, eschatology, and ethics.

The body of the instruction, at least as seen from one of its best preserved fragments (4Q416 2 and parallels), presents advice from a senior sage to "one who understands" (one who needs and seeks understanding). The individual units generally begin with second-person singular imperative or a prohibition ("you shall not"). Much of the work's content is typical of Jewish wisdom literature as seen in Proverbs and Sirach. There are treatments of money matters, social relations, and family issues. The one being instructed is told to pay back loans quickly, to free himself as soon as possible from the legal obligations connected with guaranteeing the loans

---

[5] See Daniel J. Harrington, *Wisdom Texts from Qumran* (London: Routledge, 1996). For the full text see the edition by John Strugnell and Daniel J. Harrington, *Qumran Cave 4*. Vol. 24, *Sapiential Texts, Part 2. 4QInstruction.* Discoveries in the Judaean Desert 34 (Oxford: Clarendon Press, 1999).

of others and holding deposits for them, and to cultivate a moderate lifestyle. He should preserve his independence from others while seeking to please his superiors and refraining from asserting his superiority over his inferiors. The treatment of family matters often uses biblical texts as starting points and makes them part of the wisdom instruction. Thus it considers why and how the prospective sage should honor his parents (in light of Exod 20:12; Deut 5:16), exercise dominion over his wife (with reference to Gen 2:24 and 3:16), and annul his wife's vows and votive offerings (on the basis of Num 30:6-15).

The same basic format and similar concerns appear in another substantial instruction preserved in 4Q417 2 and parallels. This section deals with sensitivity in correcting others, warns against associating with evildoers, cautions against greed and delighting in the misfortunes of others, gives counsel about maintaining one's integrity, and provides further advice on financial matters.

These instructions are punctuated by calls to study or contemplate "the mystery that is to be/come" *(rāz nihyeh),* which will lead to knowing "all the ways of truth . . . and all the roots of iniquity." One who meditates on this mystery will gain ethical knowledge (about "truth and iniquity, wisdom and foolishness"), an understanding of the cosmos ("by the *rāz nihyeh* He has laid out its foundation"), and a vision of the future ("what is to be"). Using the motif of the heavenly tablets (see Exod 32:20-22), the instructor warns: "Engraved is the ordinance, and ordained are all the punishments." The heavenly tablets apparently contain a list of evil deeds and the consequences or punishments that follow upon them at the judgment.

The precise nature of the "mystery" remains elusive. It is probably not identical with the Torah, nor is it necessarily a particular book (the "Book of Meditation," or the "Rule of the Community"). Rather, it seems to be analogous to the New Testament concept of the "kingdom of God" in that it is never precisely defined, has several dimensions (cosmic, ethical, eschatological), and is held up as the key to all knowledge and to all human activities in the present and future.

There are many other interesting items in 4QInstruction. One such feature is that the feminine singular imperatives and prohibitions in 4Q415 2 ii 1-9 indicate that here a woman is being addressed directly. We must assume that she is the wife of the male being instructed throughout most of the work. She is told to honor her father-in-law, to cling to the bosom of her husband, not to neglect the "holy covenant" (marriage), and to be the subject of praise from all men.

Another unusual feature is that the angels provide an example and a model for the righteous on earth: "Angels of holiness serve Him in heaven;

but the earth He has given over to the sons of truth" (4Q418 55 8-9). The righteous are promised as a reward for their behavior an angelic existence—meditating on God's power, glory, and faithfulness, and praising God's name forever (4Q418 126 ii), while the foolish are warned to expect the "everlasting pit" and even annihilation (4Q418 69).

Still another interesting feature is the use of agricultural imagery in several fragments (4Q418 103; 4Q423 2 and 5). Whether this imagery is to be taken literally or metaphorically is not clear, but if it is taken literally these texts would provide a contrast to Ben Sira's reflections on the trades in which the farmer (see Sir 38:24-26) is acknowledged as making an important but limited contribution to society whereas the true sage devotes himself entirely to "higher things" (Sir 39:1-11). According to 4QInstruction it is possible that a farmer may also be a sage.

The author of 4QInstruction and Ben Sira use many of the same modes of teaching: proverbs or maxims, prohibitions, instructions, and so on. Both write in a literary *persona* of a father ("my son") or more likely a senior sage instructing his students. They deal with many of the same topics: money, loans, parents, wives and children, and so on. While both use parts of the Torah in their wisdom teachings, they have different theological agendas. Ben Sira wants to integrate wisdom and Torah, even to the point of identifying them (24:23). The author of 4QInstruction, however, seeks to locate wisdom in a comprehensive theological framework—the *rāz niyheh*—that embraces creation, ethics, and eschatology. He gives special emphasis to the revelation of the mystery *(rāz)* in the future and presents his wisdom teachings as examples of the behavior that is consonant with the mystery.[6]

The Wisdom of Solomon

The book of Wisdom (or Wisdom of Solomon) is more a book about wisdom—its benefits, nature, and role in history—than a wisdom book that gives advice (like Proverbs, Qoheleth/Ecclesiastes, and Sirach). It is an exhortation to seek wisdom and live by it.[7] Although he is never named, the implicit author is again (as in Proverbs and Qoheleth) King Solomon (especially in ch. 9), and he addresses the "rulers of the earth" (1:1; see

---

[6] For a full comparison see Daniel J. Harrington, "Two Early Jewish Approaches to Wisdom: Sirach and Qumran Sapiential Work A," in Charlotte Hempel, Armin Lange, and Hermann Lichtenberger, eds., *The Wisdom Texts from Qumran and the Development of Sapiential Thought* (Leuven: Peeters, 2002) 263–75.

[7] See David Winston, *The Wisdom of Solomon*. AB 43 (Garden City, NY: Doubleday, 1979); and Michael Kolarcik, "Book of Wisdom," in *New Interpreter's Bible* (Nashville: Abingdon, 1997) 5:435–600.

also 6:1). But the real author can hardly be Solomon, since he writes in Greek and uses Stoic and Platonic philosophical ideas. And the real audience seems more likely to have been Alexandrian Jews than Gentile kings. The book is a defense of the Jewish religion as superior to other religions and philosophies. Its composition is generally placed in the first century B.C.E. in Alexandria in Egypt, which in antiquity was a great cultural center with a large Jewish population.

The three main parts of the book of Wisdom concern righteousness and immortality (chs. 1–5), wisdom (chs. 6–9), and wisdom's role in Israel's early history (chs. 10–19). While the author's chief source is the Bible, he makes extensive use of Greek philosophical ideas and rhetorical techniques. Convinced of the truth and superiority of Judaism, he criticizes the idolatry of other religions and the materialism of Epicureanism.

The first part of the book (chs. 1–5) is concerned with wisdom and righteousness. It describes wisdom in terms of the Stoic concept of the world soul: "the spirit of the Lord has filled the world, and that which holds all things together knows what is said" (1:7). And it encourages the righteous to remain faithful to their Jewish principles in the face of the plottings of the wicked. Their fidelity should be based on their belief in life after death, and in rewards and punishments in accord with one's actions during life on earth. Despite the expectations of the wicked that death marks the end of human existence, the author proclaims that "the souls of the righteous are in the hand of God, and no torment will ever touch them" (3:1). The hope of the righteous is "full of immortality" (3:4), while their sufferings are endured as a discipline (3:5-6). Their existence after death (3:7-9) is glorious ("they shine forth . . . like sparks"), and they share in God's kingdom and in God's truth, love, and merciful care. The hope of immortality put forth in Wisdom gives purpose and direction to human ethical activity, since the reward for righteous living is eternal life. It also provides an approach to the problem of innocent suffering and theodicy, since it defers the definitive display of God's omnipotence and justice to the time of death and/or the last judgment.

In the second part (chs. 6–9) "Solomon" urges kings and judges to seek for wisdom. As in Prov 8:22-31, Wisdom is personified as a female figure. In this book Wisdom is encyclopedic, embracing even the natural sciences (7:17-21), and is called "the fashioner of all things" (7:22a). In 7:22b-24 Wisdom is described in terms of twenty-one attributes ("intelligent, holy, unique, manifold, subtle, etc.") and as the world soul ("more mobile than any motion . . . she pervades and penetrates all things"; see also 1:7). Then in 7:25-26 Wisdom's close relationship with God is expressed in terms such as "breath," "emanation," "reflection," "mirror," and "image." In 7:27-28 Wisdom is said to "pass into holy souls and make them friends of God and prophets." Finally in 7:29-31 Wisdom has significance in both the moral ("against wisdom evil does not prevail") and the cosmic ("she orders all things well") spheres. Indeed, Wisdom is said to be the source of all virtues, including the classic list of cardinal virtues: "she teaches self-control and prudence, justice and courage" (8:7).

The third part (chs. 10–19) describes Wisdom's role in Israel's early history. The idea is that Wisdom was at work as the means by which God directed history from Adam to Moses. The excursus on idolatry in chapters 13–15 ridicules the practice of worshiping nature or the products of human invention, and traces all sins and vices back to idolatry: "the worship of idols . . . is the beginning and cause and end of every evil" (14:27; see Rom 1:18-32). On the contrary, "our God" is the only true God, and as such is the source of righteousness and immortality (15:1-3).

With Alexander the Great's conquest of the ancient Near East in the 4th century B.C.E., the form of Greek culture known as Hellenism made a great impact on the language, economy, military strategy, and thought of Jews both in the land of Israel and in the Diaspora. In this context Ben Sira is often regarded as a Jewish traditionalist or conservative voice with respect to Hellenism, indeed, even a resister to it. This interpretation, however, might be an exaggeration, since he may well have known and used Greek and Egyptian literary sources in his school. And the fact that his grandson felt compelled to translate his book into Greek shows how influential Hellenism was even on its alleged opponents. However, the author of the book of Wisdom clearly goes much further in embacing the language, rhetoric, and philosophical concepts of Hellenism, even while arguing for the superiority of Jewish wisdom. His acceptance of the ideas of wisdom as a world soul and of personal immortality set him apart from Ben Sira and enabled him to deal with problems (innocent suffering, retribution after death) that Ben Sira did not resolve.

The Sermon on the Mount

The Sermon on the Mount in Matthew 5–7 is surely one of the best-known parts of the Christian Bible. It contains the beatitudes (5:3-12), the Lord's Prayer (6:9-13), the reflection on the "lilies of the field" (6:28-30), and the Golden Rule (7:12). The Sermon seems to have been composed by the evangelist Matthew on the basis of various traditions from the Sayings Source Q (compare Luke 6:20-49) and other ancient collections of Jesus' teachings. Though it was put into its present Greek form by Matthew or a predecessor, there is little doubt that on many issues the Matthean version of the sermon allows us to hear the voice of Jesus the wisdom teacher.[8]

The Sermon on the Mount is the first of five great speeches by Jesus in Matthew's gospel. The other four discourses deal with the demands of discipleship (ch. 10), the kingdom of heaven (ch. 13), community life (ch. 18), and preparation for the full coming of the kingdom of God (chs. 24–25). Placed first in the series of speeches, the Sermon on the Mount serves as a summary or compendium of Jesus' most important and distinctive teachings.

Matthew's Sermon on the Mount consists of five major sections. The introduction (5:3-16) presents "beatitudes" that set forth the personal characteristics, values, attitudes, and actions that will be rewarded in the fullness of God's kingdom and are therefore to be cultivated in the present, along with a series of images (salt of the earth, light of the world, city on a hill) that express the importance of those who follow Jesus' teachings. The second part (5:17-48) affirms that Jesus came "not to abolish but to fulfill" the Law and the Prophets, and gives six examples that illustrate how he deepens and intensifies biblical teachings about murder and anger, adultery and lust, marriage and divorce, oaths, retaliation and nonviolence, and love of enemies. The third part (6:1-18) deals with the right ways and the wrong ways to perform three key acts of piety: almsgiving, prayer, and fasting. The fourth part (6:19–7:12) provides wise advice about various topics: treasures, eyes, masters, anxiety, judgments, dogs and pigs, prayer, and the Golden Rule. The final exhortation (7:13-27) offers short parables about gates and ways, trees and fruits, and houses and foundations to emphasize the challenges involved in practicing Jesus' teachings and the need for personal integrity and spiritual depth.

Given the Jewish roots of Jesus and Matthew in Judaism and the Jewish character of the teaching, it seems that the best literary analogies for the Sermon on the Mount are to be found among the wisdom instructions in Proverbs, Qoheleth/Ecclesiastes, and Sirach. The content includes general principles, attitudes, and actions. It uses the literary forms employed by Jewish wisdom teachers: beatitudes, proverbs, commands and prohibitions, reasons or motives ("for . . ."), general principles, parables, and so forth. As in the Jewish wisdom instructions, the sermon moves from topic to topic often on the basis of key words or themes rather than offering an extended argument or a logical development.

In form and content it appears that the Sermon on the Mount is best viewed as a wisdom instruction. As such the sermon is best taken as part of

---

[8] See Daniel J. Harrington, *The Gospel of Matthew.* SP 1 (Collegeville: Liturgical Press, 1991) 76–111. For Jesus' place in the wisdom tradition see Ben C. Witherington, *Jesus the Sage: The Pilgrimage of Wisdom* (Minneapolis: Fortress, 1994).

an ethics of character or virtue ethics. The horizon and goal is the kingdom of God. The content tells people how to prepare to enjoy the fullness of God's kingdom and how to act appropriately in the present. The search for perfection takes God as its model and criterion: "Be perfect, therefore, as your heavenly Father is perfect" (5:48). Its ethical teachings are part of a narrative in which Jesus is both the master teacher and the best example of his own teaching. Being a disciple in Jesus' wisdom school involves formation in character and commitment to certain ways of acting. Rather than providing a complete code of conduct, the Sermon on the Mount seeks to form Christians to discern wisely and to act correctly. It presupposes life in community and the community's positive impact on the common good.

Matthew's gospel is a long narrative about the life, death, and resurrection of Jesus of Nazareth. The wisdom instruction presented in the Sermon on the Mount is only a small part (three out of twenty-eight chapters) of the gospel. However, in form and content the sermon sounds much like parts of Sirach. Both wisdom instructions presuppose the literary *persona* of a wise teacher—Jesus of Nazareth and Jesus Ben Sira. But whereas Ben Sira presents himself as a wisdom teacher only, Matthew suggests at several points that Jesus of Nazareth was Wisdom incarnate (see Matt 11:19, 25-30; 23:37-39). Moreover, while both teachers use the Torah in their wisdom teachings, Matthew claims that by going to the root of the Torah Jesus has "fulfilled" it (see Matt 5:17-48) and so brought it to its goal at a new level. Finally, Matthew's Jesus places all his wise teachings in the context of the coming kingdom of God and promises eschatological rewards to those who act in accord with the demands of God's kingdom.

The Letter of James

The New Testament writing attributed to "James" is traditionally regarded as a letter, mainly because it contains in its opening verse a reference to the sender (James) and the addressees ("the twelve tribes in the Dispersion") along with a greeting. However, the so-called letter is really a wisdom instruction much like Sirach in form and content. The writer imparts advice on a wide range of topics in no apparent logical order. His message is intensely practical: "But be doers of the word, and not merely hearers who deceive themselves" (1:22).[9]

The implied author is James, a relative of Jesus (his brother, stepbrother, or cousin?) who was prominent in the early Jerusalem church and suffered

---

[9] See Patrick J. Hartin, *James*. SP 14 (Collegeville: Liturgical Press, 2003); and idem, *James of Jerusalem*. Interfaces (Collegeville: Liturgical Press, 2004).

a martyr's death in 62 C.E. If this James was the real author, then this wisdom instruction would be a very early Christian document representing the concerns of a Palestinian Jewish Christian teacher for those outside the land of Israel ("the Dispersion," or Diaspora). But most scholars regard it as a somewhat later (80 C.E. or so) work written in James' name and emanating from a "James" school or circle somewhere in the eastern Mediterranean world.

James mentions Jesus only twice, and then only in formulaic (though exalted) terms: "Lord Jesus Christ" (1:1; 2:1). His interests lay not in christology or theology but in giving practical advice on many matters. He defines religion as "to care for orphans and widows in their distress, and to keep oneself unstained by the world" (1:27). In a culture in which religion was generally defined in terms of rituals, temples, and material sacrifices, this definition was unusual and even revolutionary.

A major concern in James' wisdom instruction is what we might call "social justice." Early on he warns that the rich will be brought low and disappear like flowers in the field (1:9-11). In 2:1-13 he criticizes favoritism or partiality toward the rich and discrimination against the poor and insists on equal treatment for all. He goes on to defend what might be called the preferential option for the poor: "Has not God chosen the poor in the world to be rich in faith and to be heirs of the kingdom" (2:5). Then he rails against the rich who oppress the poor and drag them into court.

The most famous part of the letter of James is the reflection on faith and works in 2:14-26. Here James takes issue with a distorted version of Paul's doctrine of justification by faith. James insists on both faith and works, since "faith by itself, if it has no works, is dead" (2:17). He even interprets Abraham as the exemplar not of faith alone (compare Galatians 3 and Romans 4) but rather of faith and works, and as proof that "a person is justified by works and not by faith alone" (2:24). Whether the object of James' polemic was Paul himself is not clear. But what is clear is that James promotes a kind of Christianity with deep roots in the Jewish wisdom tradition.

In chapter 3 James deals extensively with the topic of speech, a favorite topic of Jewish wisdom teachers like Ben Sira. James regards avoiding mistakes in speaking as the key to self-control and harmonious living (3:1-5a), and he describes the errant tongue as a fire capable of setting ablaze a forest (3:5b-6). In chapter 4 he traces conflicts and disputes to the passions that wage war within the person.

In 4:13-17 James returns to the topic of money, and in particular the plans of merchants to make lots of money in the near future. He reminds them that they may not live even into tomorrow and so all their plans may go up in smoke. This reflection (compare Luke 12:16-21) launches James into a tirade against the rich in chapter 5: "Come now, you rich people, weep and wail for the miseries coming to you" (5:1). He accuses the rich of withholding the wages of their workers (5:4), of living in luxury (5:5), and of condemning and murdering righteous persons who resist them (5:6). He urges the poor to be patient until the coming of the Lord, when God's justice will be made fully manifest (5:7-8).

As a part of the Christian canon of Holy Scripture, the letter of James carries on the tradition of the wisdom books contained in the Old Testament. It insists that Christians be "doers of the word" and so put their beliefs into practice and let them have an impact on what they do. As such, this wise little book is an important part of the Christian Bible.

James and Sirach are alike in their literary form and their content. The almost total lack of explicit christology in James makes the similarities seem even more impressive. Ben Sira shares James' interest in suffering as a discipline, caution in speech, and concern with money matters. Both writers can be described as proponents of social justice, though the fiery words of James on this topic go beyond anything in the book of Sirach. But James clearly addresses members of a Christian community, not students in a wisdom school or the equivalent in the readership for which Ben Sira wrote.

Conclusion

Where does Ben Sira stand in relation to the other books in the category of ancient Jewish wisdom books? In form and content Ben Sira agrees with much that is in Proverbs and may well have used it as a source. In particular, he generally upholds the law of retribution and does not appeal to life after death as the solution to the problem of theodicy. His most obvious advance on Proverbs comes in his better integration of biblical traditions (especially from the Torah) with ancient Near Eastern wisdom traditions.

Ben Sira displays little of the critical theological acumen manifested in the book of Job and does not share the pessimism that permeates Qoheleth/Ecclesiastes. Indeed, some scholars regard Sirach as a positive and constructive response to the negativism of Qoheleth. While Ben Sira shares an instructional style and some content with 4QInstruction, he shows little or no interest in the eschatology associated with "the mystery that is to be/come," which serves as an important theological horizon for the Qumran text.

The book of Wisdom stands apart from Sirach in its willingness to use Greek philosophical concepts, its identification of Wisdom as the world soul, and its emphasis on life after death and vindication for the wise and righteous. None of these features is prominent in Sirach.

While Sirach is similar in form and content to the Sermon on the Mount in Matthew 5–7, what sets the wisdom instruction of Jesus of Nazareth apart from that of Jesus Ben Sira is the former's appeal to the coming kingdom of God as the horizon of his ethical teachings. However, Sirach is an excellent resource for the exposition of the letter of James and vice versa. Apart from the two mentions of "Lord Jesus Christ" (1:1; 2:1) and the closing references to Christian community life, the wisdom instruction attributed to James has a great deal in common with Sirach in terms of form and content. Now we can give closer scrutiny to Ben Sira's book.

CHAPTER THREE

Reading Ben Sira's Book

My guess is that most readers of this volume have never read Ben Sira's book from start to finish. Catholics may have heard short selections from it at liturgies. Protestant and Jewish readers may be even less familiar with it, since Sirach is not a part of their Sacred Scriptures. Furthermore, Ben Sira's book is not easy to read. It comes from long ago and far way. But the principal reason for its difficulty is that it is an anthology, a collection of short units gathered together without much apparent logical order. Most of us are not in the habit of reading anthologies of poetry or short stories from cover to cover. Rather, we pick and choose at our leisure. Moreover, Ben Sira does not tell a story, as the authors of the books of Genesis or of Samuel and Kings do. Nor does he supply a narrative framework for his own wise teachings, as the evangelists do for the wisdom of Jesus.

Those who are not familiar with Ben Sira's book will need a guide before they can move on to the more specialized topics treated in the remaining chapters in this book. What follows is meant to provide a map for beginners in their reading of Sirach and a reference resource to consult as they continue working with this book. The exposition of individual passages that follows seeks to open up the book of Sirach on the literary, historical, and theological levels.[1] However, the reading guide is not a substitute for reading and reflecting on the text itself. Rather, it seeks to enrich and

---

[1] What follows is a shortened and revised version of my article on Sirach in *The International Bible Commentary*, ed. William R. Farmer (Collegeville: Liturgical Press, 1998) 923–50. James L. Crenshaw provides a more extensive (and excellent) exposition in "Sirach," *New Interpreter's Bible* (Nashville: Abingdon, 1997) 5:601–867. The best scholarly commentary is by Patrick W. Skehan and Alexander A. Di Lella, *The Wisdom of Ben Sira.* AB 39 (Garden City, NY: Doubleday, 1987).

stimulate that reading and reflection. On the literary level it calls attention to the narrative situation (Ben Sira instructing his student), literary and rhetorical devices, striking images and expressions, and progress of thought or logical structure. On the historical level it points out social or cultural assumptions (about women, slavery, the household, etc.) that are needed for a fair, if not sympathetic, reading. Since Ben Sira's comments about contemporary events around 180 B.C.E. in Jerusalem are at best allusive, little effort will be given to trying to make them explicit. On the theological level it tries to indicate where Ben Sira stood on particular issues, with special attention to biblical sources and parallels.

In reading through the book of Sirach you might pay special attention to the theological context of wisdom and fear of the Lord that Ben Sira constructs for all his wise teachings. Within that framework you might then notice how Ben Sira treats the standard topics found in other wisdom books: happiness, social relations, money and possessions, justice, family life, the household, friendship, honor and shame, discipline and self-control, death, and so on. Look also for how Ben Sira treats theological topics (sin, forgiveness, etc.) and how he integrates wisdom teachings and legal statements found in the Torah. From a careful reading of the text Ben Sira will emerge as a writer with an eye for parallel formulations (so we always get the point) and for intricate structures (the better to memorize). And of course, prepare yourself for the grand vision presented in the final chapters in which Ben Sira reflects on how God's glory is made manifest in creation (42:15–43:33) and in Israel's history (44:1–50:24).

1:1-30: The Origin and Nature of Wisdom. Where does wisdom come from? What is it? How does one get it? The initial poem (1:1-10) deals with those issues first by making statements and asking questions (1:1-3, 4-6) and then by developing the theme of God as the origin of wisdom (1:8-10). The truly wise one created all wisdom and gives it to those who love him. Wisdom appears as a female creature, as in Prov 8:22-31; she is later identified with the Torah (see 24:23). The proper response to God's gift of Wisdom (1:11-20) involves fear of the Lord: the respect, gratitude, and right behavior that are owed to the Creator of all wisdom. The poem celebrating fear of the Lord first reflects on the good results of fearing the Lord (1:11-13) and then praises fear of the Lord as the beginning (1:14-15), fullness (1:16-17), crown (1:18-19), and root (1:20) of wisdom. The portrayal of wisdom as a female personal figure is continued, and so is the emphasis on wisdom as a gift from God. Though Ben Sira probably did not believe in life after death, his comment in 1:13 about the sage being blessed on the day of his death at least prepares for such a belief. The section contrasting unjustified anger and patience (1:22-24) operates on the level of practical wisdom and gives particular attention to the consequences of such behaviors. The second section (1:25-27) brings together Ben Sira's major theological interests: the connection between wisdom, fear of the Lord, discipline, and keeping the commandments. Thus he links the secular wisdom tradition exemplified in 1:22-24 and Israel's religious tradition, especially the Torah. The third section (1:28-30) joins practical wisdom teachings regarding integrity vis-à-vis God and humans with a warning that God will surely expose and bring shame upon the hypocrite.

2:1-18: Fear of the Lord. The six short units in this chapter explore various facets of fear of the Lord or "faith" in the sense of fidelity toward God. Fear of the Lord is Ben Sira's integrating theme; it brings together faith and works, knowledge of God and behavior, love of God and love of neighbor, and so forth. The center of the chapter is the affirmation that "the Lord is compassionate and merciful; he forgives sins and saves in time of distress" (2:11). Because God is merciful, one should be respectful and faithful. The concluding confession (absent in the Greek but present in other texts), "equal to his name are his works," assumes that God's name is "the merciful one" *(raḥum)*. Biblical "fear" and "faith" are based on the character and experience of God the compassionate one. The first unit (2:1-6) warns one who would try to be faithful to God to expect "testing" (a powerful biblical theme), and to remain trusting and hopeful despite temporary or apparent humiliations. It explains suffering as a discipline: "For gold is tested in the fire, and those found acceptable in the furnace of humiliation" (2:5; see Prov 3:11-12; 17:3; 27:21; Wis 3:6; Jas 1:12; 1 Pet 1:7). The second unit (2:7-9) addresses "you who fear the Lord" and echoes the first unit (see 2:6) with commands to "trust" ("believe") in God and "hope" for good things. The questions in the third unit (2:10-11) are based on Pss 22:4-5 and 37:25, though the book of Job calls into question the easy "yes" answers Ben Sira expects. For the Lord as "compassionate and merciful" see Exod 34:6, and as "forgiving" sins and "saving" see Pss 37:39-40; 103:3; 145:18-19. By way of contrast, the fourth unit (2:12-14) features three "woes" (warnings or threats) against the timid and sinners. The Lord's "reckoning" mentioned in 2:14 most likely refers in Sirach to events within the person's lifetime, though other Jewish and Christian texts use the same vocabulary to describe the Last Judgment. Taking up the language of 2:7-9, the fifth unit (2:15-17) describes the characteristics of "those who fear the Lord." The final verse (2:18) prefers the lordship of God to that of human beings because God is the merciful one. The first two chapters, with their reflections on the origin and nature of wisdom and on the faithful service of

God ("fear of the Lord"), provide the theological framework for the rest of the book.

3:1-16: Parents and Children. How fear of the Lord expresses itself in family relationships is illustrated by the precept "Honor your father and your mother" (Exod 20:12; Deut 5:16). Addressing adult children ("my sons") rather than youngsters, Ben Sira uses wisdom traditions to explain the reasons for as well as the results and advantages that follow upon honoring one's parents. His teachings expand on the biblical promise "so that your days may be long and that it may go well for you" (Deut 5:16). The fundamental reason why children should honor both parents is the social order decreed by God that places parents in authority over their children (3:1-2). A series of participial phrases ("those who . . ." 3:3-7) describes the spiritual blessings that come from honoring parents: atonement for sins, spiritual treasures, long and happy life, and so on. These instructions associate respect for and from parents with honor and shame (3:8-11), and promise that caring for parents in their old age will be rewarded by God ("credited to you against your sins," 3:12-15). The poem ends (3:16) by returning to 3:2, and warns that neglect of father and mother is blasphemy.

3:17-29: Humility. The first section (3:17-20) concerns humility (or "meekness") in action, and the remaining two units (3:21-24; 3:25-29) warn against intellectual pride. Those who act humbly will be loved by others (who loves an arrogant person?) and by God (since wise persons recognize their own limits and the unlimited glory of God). The warnings against intellectual pride are often read against the background of Ben Sira's conflict with Hellenistic philosophy and culture around 200 B.C.E. But they apply to people of any age and are presented here as general statements. The true sources of wisdom are "what you have been commanded" (3:22; see Qoh 12:13) and the wisdom tradition (3:29). Those who neglect the Torah and wisdom to meddle in things beyond them go astray; they thus display a "hard heart" that ends in destruction.

3:30–4:10: Almsgiving. Though giving to the poor was not a part of Greek wisdom, it was an important element in the Jewish tradition (see Tobit). These instructions presuppose that the sage has wealth and so is in a position to play the role of benefactor. For the ideal sage as benefactor see Job's self-portrait in Job 29. The first unit (3:30-31) gives reasons for almsgiving: atonement for sins and widening one's circle of friends. The second unit (4:1-6) lists ten things not to do when giving alms, and adds a reason for avoiding these actions (God will heed the curse of the rejected beggar). The third unit (4:7-10) contains general teachings about how the sage should behave in society and especially about his obligations to the poor, oppressed, orphaned, and widowed. The instruction ends with a promise that the charitable person will be "like a son of the Most High" and especially loved by God (more than by his mother!).

4:11-19: The Benefits of Wisdom. As in chapter 1, wisdom appears as a personal figure, an intermediary between God and humans. The first unit (4:11-14) lists the benefits of seeking wisdom: instruction and help, life, joy, glory, and blessing from God. In the Greek text there is an alternation between singular and plural participles: "whoever loves her . . . those who seek her." The Hebrew text of the second (4:15-16) and third (4:17-19) units presents wisdom as the speaker ("those who obey me, I will hand them over"). The rewards listed in 4:15-16 probably pertain to this world. Despite its many rewards, the way of wisdom involves testing (see 2:1) and discipline (4:17-19). Those who persevere on wisdom's way will find joy and knowledge; those who do not will end in destruction. Underlying all these rewards is the conviction that serving wisdom is the same as serving the Holy One.

4:20–6:4: Honor and Shame. The five units display an interlocking or concentric outline: A, the need for self-restraint (4:20-21); B, truthful speech (4:22-31); C, avoiding presumption (5:1-8); B', truthful speech (5:9–6:1); A', the need for self-restraint (6:2-4). The first unit (4:20-21) places the instructions in the framework of honor and shame. The key word is "self" or "soul" *(psychē),* and the sage is told to exercise restraint and discernment in which fear of shame can play a salutary role. The second unit (4:22-31) consists mainly of "do not" clauses concerned with speech as a major element in social relations ("wisdom becomes known through speech," 4:24), along with instructions about not showing partiality (4:22, 27), fighting for the truth (4:28), and generosity (4:31). The central unit (5:1-8) is framed by sayings about not relying on wealth (5:1-2, 8) and focuses on presumptuous attitudes toward God (5:3-7). These attitudes include denying God's power over oneself, presuming on God's forbearance and mercy, and putting off repentance. These postures reflect the excuses commonly put forward by sinners, though there may also be a criticism of Greek philosophical schools or even Qoheleth. The theme of truthful speech is taken up again in the fourth unit (5:9–6:1), where the key word is "double-tongued" *(diglossos,* 5:9, 14; 6:1) or "slanderer." The saying about being quick to hear and slow to answer is found also in Jas 1:19. In the second part (5:13–6:1) honor and shame appear as motives for avoiding "double-tongued" behavior. The final unit (6:2-4) takes up again the key word of the first unit, "self" or "soul" *(psychē).* Ben Sira's anthropology is not exactly the same as those of the ancient Greeks or of people today. For him the soul is the life-principle (Hebrew *nepeš*). An evil soul destroys its possessor and brings shame. The sage who follows all these instructions will stay out of trouble with respect to others and to God.

6:5-17: Friendship. Ben Sira provides the most extensive treatment of friendship in the Bible (see also 9:10-16; 19:13-17; 22:19-26; 27:16-21; 37:1-6). His approach is not theoretical, nor is he much concerned with the definition of friendship or why people need friends. Rather he offers practical advice about making friends and warns against fair-weather friends. After holding up pleasant speech as a way of attracting friends (6:5), he counsels a cautious attitude (6:6-7, 13) toward friends and gives a series of examples about false friends (6:8-12) who quickly fall away in times of trouble and testing. However, true friends (6:14-17) are like a shelter, treasure, and lifesaving medicine; they are to be found especially among those "who fear the Lord."

6:18-37: Discipline as the Way to Wisdom. The three units in this section (6:18-22, 23-31, 32-37) begin with "my child" and advise the young sage to accept "discipline" *(musar)*—the kind of intellectual and moral formation that produces wisdom and its rewards. The first unit (6:18-22) contrasts those who accept discipline (like farmers who work and then enjoy a rich harvest) and those who reject it (for them it is like a heavy stone). Discipline is "like her name" (6:22) in that fools "cast it aside" (a play on *musar,* meaning "discipline," and the Hebrew verb *sur,* meaning "turn aside"). After a call to pay attention (6:23), the second unit develops the image of discipline as a "yoke" that binds the whole body (6:24-25), moves to images of searching and hunting (6:26-28), and shows how the yoke is then transformed into glorious apparel (6:29-31). What discipline gives is wisdom, which results in "rest" and "joy" (6:28; see 51:27-28). The third unit (6:32-37) directs the young sage to spend time with wise elders and to listen to their discourse and proverbs as the way of becoming wise. This kind of intellectual discipline would be typical of ancient Near Eastern wisdom writings. Ben Sira's distinctively Jewish approach to discipline and wisdom emerges in 6:37: The prospective sage must attend to the commandments of God and recognize God as the source of wisdom. For Ben Sira "discipline" includes not only tested human wisdom but also (and especially) the Torah.

7:1-17: Avoiding Evil. This passage (and what follows) represents the practical advice expressed in the "godly discourse" and "wise proverbs" that constitute the discipline of the sage. Each of the sixteen units, except the last (7:17), begins with a negative command: "Do not." The topics include avoiding evil and injustice (7:1-3), ambition for high offices and public recognition (7:4-7), presuming on God's patience and mercy (7:8-9), carelessness in speech (7:10-14), and other matters (7:15-17). The pieces of advice are sometimes accompanied by theological motives about the sovereignty of God (7:11), the evil effects of injustice (7:3) and lying (7:13), and the threat of punishment (7:17). In the Hebrew text the punishment is simply "the worm" (= death), while in the Greek it is "fire and worms" (perhaps an indication of the grandson's belief in punishments after death).

7:18-36: Social Relations. These instructions are directed specifically to the male head of a household—one that includes slaves (7:20-21), cattle (7:22), children (7:23-25), a wife or wives (7:19, 26), and parents (7:27-28). The man of means and power also has obligations to friends (7:18), the priests of God (7:29-31), and the needy (7:32-35). The instructions assume that slaves can gain their freedom (Exod 21:2; Lev 25:39-43; Deut 15:12-15), that marriages of daughters are arranged by their fathers (7:25), that only the husband can initiate divorce (7:19, 26; see Deut 24:1-4), and that priests deserve their portion (7:29-31; see Num 18:9-20). The motivations for acting in the "right" way range from self-interest (harmony, avoiding trouble, good reputation) to obligations imposed from outside (parents, God).

8:1-19: Caution in Social Relations. The form in which the advice about persons and situations the sage should avoid is given consists of a command ("Do not . . .") and a reason why the person or situation is to be avoided. The reasons are mainly pragmatic (avoiding harm or disgrace), though the motive clauses in 8:5-7 are more spiritual or philosophical. At the center of the text is the command to attend to the discourse of the sages (8:8) and the elders (8:9), thus stressing the traditional character of this wisdom based on human experience. The kinds of persons to be avoided—powerful, rich, loudmouths, ill-bred, sinners, insolent, and so on—have the power to work harm to the sage. Even those who seem powerless—repentant sinners, the old, the dead—can be occasions for disgrace unless the sage acts cautiously. For the sage whose social status and personal identity are closely intertwined, the attitude of prudent calculation in dealing with others—especially those who can cause harm—is most appropriate. One element in protecting one's social position is the avoidance of self-revelation to fools and strangers (8:17-19). The relation between social and personal identity is a major concern among the sages.

9:1-9: Relations with Women. The addressee here (as everywhere in Sirach) is a young man who wants to become a sage. The advice to him about women follows the form (command plus reason) and the tone (calculating caution) of the preceding passage. Whereas in Proverbs 1–9 "loose women" tend to represent Dame Folly, here the advice concerns various types of real women who can bring harm and disgrace to the prospective sage: a jealous wife, a dominating woman, a loose woman, a songstress, a virgin, a prostitute, a beauty, and another man's wife. The Old Testament penalties for seducing a virgin (9:5) involved a financial payment to her father and marriage (Exod 22:16-17; Deut 22:29), and for adultery with another man's wife (9:9), death (Lev 20:10; Deut 22:22).

9:10-16: Friendships. This section begins with a word of caution regarding new friends (9:10) expressed in a chiastic pattern: old friends, new friends, new wine, old wine. Then it lists (9:11-13) three kinds of persons to be avoided as friends—sinners, the ungodly, and those who have the power to kill—along with reasons why they should be avoided. Those who are to be pursued as friends (9:14-16)—the wise, intelligent, and righteous—share the sage's concern for the Law of the Most High and fear of the Lord. True friendship is found "in the Lord"—where friends share common spiritual ideals (see 6:5-17).

9:17–10:5: Wise Rulers. The good ruler is the wise ruler. The unit begins (9:17) and ends (10:5) with images of "hands"—those of the artisans and of the Lord. It identifies wise words as the "tools" of the good ruler (9:17-18), reflects on the positive effects that a wise ruler has on the city's inhabitants (10:1-3), and traces the ruler's wisdom and success back to "the hand of the Lord" (10:4-5). If the good ruler is wise, then the one most competent to rule is the sage (who knows wisdom). Ben Sira trained sages to take an active role in the affairs of state (see 38:32-34).

10:6-18: Pride. The sage should avoid pride and the insolent behavior that flows from it, because pride is hateful to God and other humans, and because it has disastrous effects (10:6-8). The development of these ideas is related to the preceding section on rulers (see 10:8, 10, 13b-17). Death is the great equalizer among humans and the ultimate source of humiliation, since all human arrogance and pride end in corruption (10:9-11). The third section (10:12-18) begins by tracing the origin of pride to a deliberate turning away from God (= sin) in 10:12-13a and ends by denying that God or nature is the source of pride in 10:18. In between (10:13b-17), it reflects on how God puts down the proud and powerful and raises up the humble and lowly (see 1 Sam 2:1-10). Because pride means turning from God, God is not on the side of the proud and such persons can expect disastrous results.

10:19–11:6: Honor and Shame. In Ben Sira's world honor and shame derived from one's social standing and what other people thought of one. Those who had wealth and power were regarded as the most important; those who had neither could easily be despised. This reflection on true glory follows neatly from the preceding section on pride. The basic principle appears in 10:19: Those who fear the Lord are worthy of honor; those who transgress the Lord's commandments deserve dishonor. Various aspects of this principle are developed in short units: fear of the Lord and wisdom as the sources of true glory (10:20-25), avoiding boasting (10:26-27), humility (10:28-29), honor for the wise and the rich (10:30-31), wisdom as the source of honor (11:1), not judging by appearances (11:2-3), not boasting about fine clothes (11:4), and the reversals that befall kings (11:5-6). The reflection redefines what brings glory to a person. Instead of wealth and power, the sources of true honor and glory are knowledge, wisdom, fear of the Lord, and keeping the commandments—a combination of practical human wisdom and Jewish theology.

11:7-28: True Wealth. The section begins with a brief unit (11:7-9) about discretion in dealing with others; it may be taken either as an introduction to what follows or simply an independent piece. The remaining short units all concern God as the real source of wealth and warn against the false security of earthly riches (11:10-13, 14-19, 20-21, 22-24, 25-28). There are repeated warnings about presuming on one's efforts to amass wealth and thereby to guarantee security (11:10-11, 18-19, 20-21a, 23-24) along with reminders that God retains power over wealth and security (11:12, 14, 17, 21b, 22). Two wise observations stand out: the attitude of the "rich fool" whose security is robbed by death (11:19; see Qoh 2:21; 4:8; 5:12-14; Luke 12:16-2l), and our selective memories regarding prosperity and adversity (11:25). Over human efforts at acquiring wealth there is the shadow of death (11:19, 26-28). Since true wealth is wisdom and fear of the Lord, true character becomes manifest only at the time of death ("Call no one happy before his death"). Though many instinctively read these texts as referring to life after death, Ben Sira may have been only referring to the person's reputation and physical descendants.

11:29–12:18: Caution in Social Relations. Those persons pose danger to the sage who have the power to make his life miserable. Therefore the sage should exercise great caution in letting strangers into his household (11:29-34), in acts of kindness and beneficence (12:1-7), and in dealing with enemies (12:8-18). The three sections assume that social relations are full of danger even (and especially) for those who approach them with good will. The first section assumes that the sage is head of the household and warns that a scoundrel can ruin the sage's reputation and turn his own household against him. The second section urges caution in almsgiving and restricts the recipients to the good, devout, and humble on the grounds that "the Most High hates sinners" (12:6). The third section suggests that nearly everyone be treated as a potential enemy (12:8) and reflects on how the enemy will behave in the sage's adversity. Therefore the sage should always be on guard, even if the enemy seems to be friendly: "Who pities a snake charmer when he is bitten?" (12:13). The calculating caution proposed in this unit contrasts with Near Eastern ideals of hospitality and almsgiving. The viewpoint is pragmatic and experiential.

13:1-24: Rich and Poor. In a context in which wealth was pursued and riches were regarded as a divine blessing, Ben Sira urges caution in cultivating the rich. His basic principle is that wisdom and fear of the Lord are far more important than one's economic status. The first section (13:1-7) reflects on the dangers of trying to befriend the rich, for they will exploit and discard you. Two memorable images appear in 13:1-2: "Whoever touches pitch gets dirty . . . how can the clay pot associate with the iron kettle?" The second section (13:8-13) begins and ends with calls to caution and gives advice about dealing with a "powerful" person in a reserved and guarded manner. The third section (13:15-20) considers the fundamental incompatibility of rich and poor with the help of images from the animal kingdom (wolf/lamb, hyena/dog, wild asses/lions). The fourth section (13:21-23) compares the favorable treatment given to the rich and the unfavorable treatment of the poor. People support and make excuses for the rich, but criticize and dismiss the poor (see Jas 2:1-4). Though Ben Sira was no social revolutionary, he described sharply the dangers posed by riches to those who seek wisdom and fear of the Lord.

13:25–14:19: Using Money. The first section (13:25–14:2) reflects on the relation between the "heart" (in the Bible the place of psychic activity involving thinking and feeling) and the person's external appearance (13:25-26) and happiness (14:1-2). This may simply be an independent unit, or it may introduce the following poems on internal dispositions regarding the use of money. The poem in 14:3-10 begins and ends with mentions of the "miser" who, though his whole life is devoted to money, never enjoys it and so leads the most miserable of human existences. The miser does harm to himself (14:5-6, 9) and does no conscious good to others (14:7-8). Yet in the end the miser works not for himself but for others, since when he dies his heirs will get the enjoyment of his money (14:4). The theme of death as the proper context for reflecting on the use of money is developed at length in 14:11-19. Now is the time to use your money to serve God (14:11), to help others (14:13), and to enjoy yourself (14:11, 14), because you cannot do so after death, when your estate will be taken over by others. The section ends with a beautiful meditation on death and the changing of generations (14:17-19).

14:20–15:10: Seeking and Finding Wisdom. The two sections concern the search for wisdom (14:20-27) and the benefits of wisdom (15:1-10). The first poem begins with a beatitude (14:20-21) that declares the wise person happy or blessed in terms based on Prov 3:13, 17. The search for wisdom is portrayed with three patterns of imagery: the hunt (14:22), the house (14:23-25), and the shady tree (14:26-27). The "house of wisdom" image appears also in Prov 8:32-35; in this context it may allude to Ben Sira's wisdom school (see 51:23-28). The second poem begins (15:1) by linking fear of the Lord, the Law, and wisdom—the essential elements of Ben Sira's theology. Wisdom, portrayed as a female figure (15:2-6), will shower benefits on the wise, including the "bread of learning" and the "water of wisdom" as well as "an everlasting name" (immortality by memory). On the other hand, wisdom has nothing to do with fools and sinners (15:7-8). Only the wise can praise God properly (15:9-10); sinners cannot do so.

15:11-20: Free Will and Sin. Though some Old Testament texts may suggest that God makes people sin (see Exod 11:10; 2 Sam 24:1), Ben Sira vigorously denies it at the beginning (15:11-13) and end (15:18-20) of the passage. There is a fundamental incompatibility between the wise God and human sin. In one of the most important parts of his book Ben Sira emphasizes human freedom in the face of good and evil (15:14-17). The freedom in which God created humankind (Genesis 1–2) remains the privilege of all human beings. Ben Sira pays no attention here to "original sin"—whether it be Adam's sin (Gen 3:1-24; Rom 5:12-21) or that of the "sons of God" (Gen 6:1-4; *1 Enoch* 1–36). Instead he focuses on the human "inclination" or *yeṣer*—the disposition internal to the person that may incline toward good or evil. For Ben Sira, free will can overcome all moral obstacles: "If you choose, you can keep the commandments" (15:15). The extremes— fire and water, life and death (see Deut 30:15-20)—are matters of human choice, and so is everything in between. Ben Sira's rejection of God's role in sin and his stress on the *yeṣer* as the seat of sin are nicely paralleled in Jas 1:13-16.

16:1-23: Human Responsibility and the Effects of Sin. Having insisted that keeping the commandments and sin are matters of individual free will, Ben Sira, in four loosely related sections, takes up issues of collective and individual responsibility for sin. Whereas in biblical times many children were regarded as a divine blessing, Ben Sira in 16:1-4 insists on quality ("one can do better than a thousand") that depends on "fear of the Lord." This reflection leads into a meditation (16:5-10) on groups of sinners—the ancient giants (Gen 6:1-4), Lot's neighbors (Gen 18:16–19:29), the Canaanites, the 600,000 Israelite soldiers in the wilderness (Exod 12:37; Num 11:21)—whose evil ends came as the result of their sinfulness and stubbornness. Ben Sira's insistence on freewill and individual responsibility is clearly stated in 16:11-14: "He judges a person according to one's deeds." Thus he implies that each member of these collectives was a sinner (see Ezekiel 18; Ps 62:12). Perhaps in response to Greek philosophers or even to ideas expressed in Qoheleth and Job, Ben Sira concludes in 16:17-23 with a parody on those who claim that God is distant and has no concern for individual persons and their moral responsibility. He uses the form of a monologue in which the speaker reasons that the creator and sustainer of the universe could hardly care about one individual ("what am I in a boundless creation?"). The monologue is prefaced by the formula "Do not say" and concluded with a judgment on the folly of one who speaks such thoughts.

16:24–17:24: Creation and Responsibility for Sin. In view of the vastness of God's creation, how can an individual be held accountable for sin? Taking up the challenge of the monologue in 16:17-22, this unit contends that God has put an order into creation (16:26; 17:4) that is discernible through human reason (17:6-10) and the Law (17:11-14), and that God knows and judges the actions of every person (17:15-24). After a call to pay attention (16:24-25), the first section (16:26–17:4) uses ideas and phrases from Genesis 1–3 to describe the creation of the universe, earth, and human beings. The emphasis is on God's order and care for creation ("in an eternal order . . . they never disobey his word"). Human beings made "in his own image" (17:3) exercise dominion over the earth. The orderliness of God's creation should be recognized and celebrated by human beings through their senses, their reasoning powers, *and,* most of all, the "fear of him" that God has placed in the human heart. The proper human response to God's creation is to praise the creator (17:6-10). Moreover, the "Law of life . . . an eternal covenant" (17:11-14) adds encouragement to praise God and warning to beware of evil deeds. The Law is God's special gift to Israel and part of God's special relationship ("Israel is the Lord's own portion"). Since the monologue of l6:17-22 denied that God could be concerned with one person, in 17:15-23 Ben Sira affirms that every person's works are known to God and that "all their sins are before the Lord" (17:20). Thus the reflections on creation, human nature, and the Law converge on the conclusion that God does care about our actions and will hold us responsible for them (17:23). However, God's justice can be delayed or tempered by almsgiving (17:22) or repentance (17:24). The final mention of repentance prepares in turn for a call to repent in 17:25-32.

17:25-32: Call to Repentance. The fundamental reason for repentance is the mercy of God: "How great is the mercy of the Lord, and his forgiveness for those who return to him" (17:29). The initial call to repent (17:25-26) contains the elements of genuine repentance: turning from sin to the Lord, prayer, and hating sin. The idea that the dead in Sheol (a shadowy afterlife) cannot praise God (17:27-28; see Pss 6:5; 30:9; 88:10-12; 115:17-18; Isa 38:18) is used as a motive to repent now and praise God while you are alive. Though Ben Sira's vision of the human condition is positive, he recognizes the reality of sin that flows from human weakness and mortality (17:30, 32). If the sun can "fail" by way of an eclipse, how much more can the "inclination" and frail humanity ("dust and ashes") be expected to fail!

18:1-14: God's Majesty and Mercy. Flowing from the meditation on God's gift of creation in 16:24–17:4, the first part (18:1-7) of this unit proclaims God as the creator and the only just one, asks rhetorical questions to establish the inability of humans to express God's mighty deeds, and says that humans can hardly begin to understand God's wonders. Why then is the Lord patient and merciful toward them? Precisely because they are so weak and mortal (18:8-12), God takes pity on them and grants them forgiveness. The reflection ends (18:13-14) by contrasting the recipients of human mercy ("their neighbors") and divine mercy ("every living thing"). The merciful God is like a shepherd with his flock, a powerful image for God in the Bible. God shows compassion especially to the wise who accept his discipline and precepts (not only the traditional wisdom of the schools but also the commandments of the Torah). Therefore those who seek to become wise will be more likely to experience God's mercy.

18:15-18: Words and Gifts. Over the next few chapters Ben Sira presents wisdom sayings on various topics and gives relatively little attention to distinctively biblical themes. Moreover, the units are more anthological than logical in their literary development. The unit about words and gifts (18:15-18) introduces a major theme of the following chapters: speech (see 19:4-17; 20:1-8, 18-23, 24-31). Each of the four verses refers to words and gifts. The frame verses (18:15, 18) depict negative cases in which a good gift can be spoiled by bad words, and the center verses (18:16-17) insist that a good word is better than a gift, and that the best person offers both.

18:19-29: Reflection and Action. This unit begins (18:19a) and ends (18:29) with references to words. But the topic is more general than "before you speak, learn." The unit, on the whole, counsels the need for reflection before, during, and after action. The sage is to be "cautious in everything" (18:27) before things happen (18:19-21) and in times of plenty (18:25-26), fully aware that "all things move swiftly before the Lord." Particular attention is given to foresight in making and fulfilling vows (18:22-23) as an example of giving thought before acting. Compare the tragic story of Jephthah's vow in Judg 11:29-40.

18:30–19:3: Self-Control. Failure to exercise self-control brings disastrous results. The title of the unit, "self-control," appears in Greek and Latin manuscripts. The things needing control are the "base desires" and "appetites" related to money and sex. The focus of these reflections is the bad effects of giving in to these instincts: becoming a laughing stock to your enemies (18:31), becoming poor (18:32–19:1), being led astray by wine and loose women (19:2), and death (19:3, "decay and worms will take possession of him").

19:4-17: Gossip. Whereas a good word is better than a gift (18:16-17), loose talk is destructive not only to its subject but also to its purveyors. In 19:4-12 the prospective sage is warned against too quickly accepting slanderous tales about others (19:4-6) and against the evils of spreading gossip (19:7-9), except where it might be sinful to remain silent. Whereas the sage is admonished: "Be brave, it will not make you burst" (19:10), the gossip is compared to a woman about to give birth and to someone with an arrow stuck in his thigh (19:11-12). When a friend or neighbor is the topic of gossip, Ben Sira, in 19:13-17, recommends a direct approach. By means of a personal confrontation one may discover either that the story is false or that the friend's indiscretion is real (which then may serve as the occasion for correction and reform). The reference to letting the Law of the Most High take its course in 19:17 is probably to Leviticus 19:17-18 ("You shall love your neighbor as yourself").

19:20-30: Wisdom and Cleverness. What is the difference between wisdom and cleverness? Ben Sira's definition of true wisdom is fear of the Lord and fulfilling the Law (19:20). Without this religious foundation what may look like wisdom is, in fact, "a cleverness that is detestable" (19:23). In 19:25-28 he presents some characteristics of those whose cleverness is really guile and deceit: exact but unjust, only externally compassionate, and pretending not to notice but only waiting for an opportunity. How then can you discern between a wise person and a hypocrite? Ben Sira, in 19:29-30, suggests that a person's appearance (clothing, laughter, carriage) can provide some guidance. Though Ben Sira was a wisdom teacher, passages like this one indicate that the religious framework ("fear of the Lord") in which wisdom is learned and practiced was his criterion for distinguishing true wisdom from mere cleverness.

20:1-31: Speech. The chapter consists of small collections of sayings mainly concerned with speech. The sayings for the most part are related topically or by catchwords rather than by logical progression. The chapter is noteworthy not only for its organization by catchwords but also for its "natural" reasoning. There is no appeal to fear of the Lord and the commandments. Rather, the appeal is to human experience as the source of practical wisdom. The sayings about admonition or rebuke (20:1-3) begin with a reminder that sometimes it is wise to be silent. The idea behind 20:4 ("like a eunuch lusting to violate a girl") is apparently that a sinner cannot be forced to do what is right; it is only vaguely related to 20:3. The second unit (20:5-8) reflects on the relative merits of speech and silence in specific situations. The paradox about the silence of the wise (20:7) leads into a series of paradoxes generally concerned with gifts and money (20:9-12). The motifs of gifts and money, as well as the theme of speech and silence, are developed in 20:13-17 with particular attention to the gifts and words of the "fool." The "fool" in the wisdom tradition is deficient not only intellectually but also morally. The next unit (20:18-20) deals with types of inappropriate speech: slips of the tongue, coarse stories, and untimely proverbs from a fool. The unit on shame (20:21-23) ends with a reference to a foolish and unnecessary promise that only makes an enemy. The following unit concerns the evil of the lie and the liar (20:24-26). Though most of the chapter treats the dangers or evils related to speech, the final section (20:27-31) expresses the positive ideal of the sage who influences "the great" by articulate words (20:27-28), warns the sage against being prevented by gifts from speaking the truth (20:29), and urges the sage to speak out and not to hide wisdom (20:30-31).

21:1-10: The Destructive Power of Sin. Why avoid sin? Because it can destroy you. The address "my son" begins a new unit here and elsewhere in the book. The sage's basic advice is to stop sinning and ask for forgiveness (21:1). In the midst of the sage's warning about sin is the idea that God has a special openness to the prayers of the poor and will vindicate them (21:5). The bulk of the unit concerns the destructiveness of sin. Sin is compared (21:2-3) to a snake (see Gen 3:1-5), a lion's teeth, and a two-edged sword. Several examples (21:4, 6-8) show what happens when people build their lives on sins such as pride, arrogance, and greed. The destructive effects of sin are illustrated by two memorable figures of speech

(21:9-10): An assembly of sinners is like combustible material ("a bundle of tow") that ends in a blazing fire, and the way of sinners is smooth but ends in Sheol (the abode of the dead). Though readers familiar with Jewish apocalyptic and early Christian texts read 21:9-10 as referring to "hell," Ben Sira may simply have been commenting on the self-destructiveness of sinners and death as their "end."

21:11-28: The Sage and the Fool. The difference between the sage and the fool is developed by a series of short units (21:11-12, 13-14, 15, 16-17, 18-21, 22-24, 25-26, 27-28). Apart from 21:11 the appeal is to practical human experience, and the content can be accepted by all kinds of people. With the opening verse, however, Ben Sira equates true wisdom with keeping the Law and fear of the Lord, and thus gives the standard sapiential teachings a distinctively Jewish religious framework. It is paired with a warning that mere cleverness is not enough (21:12; see 19:24-25). The contrast between the sage and the fool is captured by the images of the life-giving spring and the broken jar (21:13-14). The contrast is especially manifest in speech (21:16-17, 25-26) and in openness to learning (21:15, 19, 21). Whereas to the fool education is like a fetter or a manacle, to the sage it is a "golden ornament" and a bracelet. They differ also in behavior, shown in their different ways of approaching a house (21:22-24). The unit ends (21:27-28) by describing two kinds of fools—one who curses another, and the slanderer—who bring even more misfortune on themselves. Thus the fool is everything the sage does not want to be.

22:1-18: Dealing with Fools. Ben Sira's basic advice about fools is avoidance. One type of fool—the idler or lazy person—is like a "filthy rock" (i.e., a stone used for wiping oneself after bowel movements) and balls of dung (22:1-2). It is especially painful when one's own children are fools (22:3-6), particularly in the case of a daughter. The uselessness of trying to deal directly with fools (22:9-10) is brought out by various images: trying to put back together a broken pot, rousing a sleeper, and telling a story to one who is drowsy. Since being dead is better than being a fool (22:11-12), the fool is even more to be pitied and mourned. The best strategy for the sage is to avoid all contact with fools (22:13) lest one suffer intellectual and moral contamination "when he shakes himself off." The burdensome character of fools is expressed in a series of comparisons (22:14-15): they are heavier than lead and harder to bear than sand, salt, and iron. The unit ends by contrasting the heart/mind of the sage (22:16-17) and of the fool (22:18).

22:19-26: Friendship. The main part of this section (22:19-22, 24) concerns ways in which friendships are destroyed—especially by "reviling, arrogance, disclosure of secrets, or a treacherous blow" (22:22). But a faithful friend (22:23, 25-26) stands by even and especially in hard times—whether it means sharing in the friend's subsequent prosperity (22:23) or suffering harm because of the friend (22:25-26). Avoiding harsh words and keeping confidences are the best ways to preserve a friendship.

22:27–23:6: Prayer and Sin. Prayers are unusual in a wisdom book in which the teacher instructs the prospective sage. This prayer (see also 36:1-22; 51:1-12) serves to introduce the following units on sins related to speech (23:7-15) and sexuality (23:16-27). Its presence reminds us of the distinctively Jewish stamp that Ben Sira places on common-stock wisdom teachings. The two parts of the prayer follow the same outline: a question (22:27; 23:2-3) and a petition addressed to God as "Father" that effectively answers the question (23:1; 23:4-6). The first part (22:27–23:1) concerns sins of the tongue, and the second part (23:2-6) deals with sins of the flesh arising from a disordered inclination *(yeṣer)*. An important motive for avoiding sin is shame before one's adversaries (23:3b). With this prayer Ben Sira acknowledges the need for God's help in avoiding sin and its consequences. The sage by himself is not fully capable of doing so.

23:7-15: Sins of Speech. The unit begins (23:7-8) with a call to listen to "instruction concerning the mouth" and a warning about the disastrous consequences of sins of the tongue. Then it focuses on oaths uttered in connection with God's name (23:9-11) and the special scrutiny they merit from God. In 23:11 there is a listing of ways one can sin through swearing oaths: too many oaths, oaths sworn in error, oaths that are disregarded, and false oaths. The final part (23:12-15) singles out some other sins of speech: blasphemy (23:12), coarse language (23:13-14), and abusive speech (23:15). The penalty for blasphemy was death (see Lev 24:16). Remembering one's parents (23:14) in the midst of a difficult social situation can restrain one from acting like a fool and thereby incurring shame. Discipline of the tongue is the key to discipline of the whole body (23:15; see Jas 3:2).

23:16-27: Sins of the Flesh. The unit begins (23:16-17) with a numerical proverb listing three kinds of sexual sins (hot passion, incest, and fornication) and warnings about their destructive effects. Then it focuses on adultery, first by the husband (23:18-21) and then by the wife (23:22-26). The psychology of the adulterer is beautifully sketched in 23:18: He fears only getting caught by human beings, whereas the One to whom he is ultimately responsible is God (23:19-20). The adulteress who bears a child by another man is guilty of offending both God and her husband (see Exod 20:14; Deut 5:18). She will suffer a public punishment and her children will not be accepted among the people of Israel. In these cases, Ben Sira assumes that sin is always punished (23:21, 24-26). The punishments of the adulterer and the adulteress underscore the central message of the entire book: "nothing is better than fear of the Lord, and nothing sweeter than to heed the commandments of the Lord" (23:27).

24:1-34: Praise of Wisdom. The approximate physical center of the book is marked by one of its most important and famous passages, consisting of personified Wisdom's praise of herself (24:1-22) and Ben Sira's comments (24:23-34). Wisdom's praise of herself (24:1-22) takes as its literary model Prov 8:22-31, which depicts Wisdom as a female figure who existed before creation and takes part in God's creative work. Ben Sira's creative contribution lay in assigning Wisdom a home in the Jerusalem Temple (24:8-12). The narrative introduction (24:1-2) describes Wisdom in female personal terms as praising herself in both earth and heaven. The female characterization may simply be grammatical, since the Hebrew *(ḥokma)* and Greek *(sophia)* words for "wisdom" are feminine nouns. Or perhaps there is an influence of a pagan female deity (Isis). The first stanza (24:3-7) in Wisdom's poem concerns the origin and activity of Wisdom. Wisdom is clearly a creature of God ("I came forth from the mouth of the Most High"). As she travels through heaven and earth, she seeks for a lasting dwelling place. Compare *1 Enoch* 42:1-3, where Wisdom finds no earthly dwelling and so returns to heaven. In the second stanza (24:8-12) Wisdom recounts how God assigned her a dwelling place in Israel at the Jerusalem Temple. Thus Ben Sira brings together the sapiential, cultic, and legal strands of Israelite piety. The comparison of Wisdom to various trees and bushes (24:13-17) emphasizes her attractiveness and lifegiving power. The final stanza (24:19-22) is an invitation to eat from Wisdom's fruits, with the observation that those who eat and drink from them will seek even more. Ben Sira's own comments (24:23-34) are introduced by his momentous equation of Wisdom and the Torah: "All this is the book of the covenant of the Most High God, the Law that Moses commanded us as an inheritance for the congregations of Jacob" (24:23; see Deut 33:4). Then he compares Wisdom to six mighty rivers (24:25-27). Note the neat literary patterns of verbs ("overflows . . . runs over . . . pours forth"), nouns ("wisdom . . . understanding . . . instruction"), and seasons ("first fruits . . . harvest . . . vintage"). So great is Wisdom that she transcends human understanding and the bounds of nature (24:28-29). In the final stanza (24:30-34) Ben Sira defines his own role as a wisdom teacher ("As for me . . ."). He develops first the river imagery ("like a canal . . . like a water channel") and then images of light ("I will again make instruction shine forth like the dawn") and prophecy ("pour out teaching"). Ben Sira the wisdom teacher is conscious of his social function of handing on the wisdom tradition to "all future generations" of those who seek wisdom (24:33b-34). See 33:16-19 for more autobiographical reflection.

25:1-11: Happiness. What kinds of people are happy? Of the three sections, two (25:1-2 and 25:7-11) are numerical proverbs. The three pleasant sights (25:1) involve harmony among people, while the three loathsome sights (25:2) concern people who do what is neither necessary nor appropriate. The reference to the old fool who commits adultery leads into an ideal picture of old age (25:3-6) marked by wisdom and fear of the Lord. The list of ten happy thoughts (25:7-11) culminates also in wisdom and fear of the Lord (25:10-11). These are the sources of genuine happiness and will bring about the other items on the list. The list in 25:8-9 features the "beatitude" form found also in the New Testament (Matt 5:3-12; Luke 6:20-23), but here in a sapiential rather than an eschatological context.

25:13–26:27: The Bad Wife and the Good Wife. Ben Sira's comments on women are notorious in many circles today. An appreciation of them demands a clear grasp of the literary setting (the experienced male teacher is instructing the young male pupil) and the cultural setting (the ideal is patriarchy, where the husband exercises oversight of the household). There are five major sections, alternating between the bad wife (25:13-26; 26:5-12) and the good wife (26:1-4; 26:13-18), and concluding with basic advice to the young sage (26:19-21) and with contrasts between bad and good women (26:22-27). The first section (25:13-26) laments the bad effects of living with an evil and angry woman ("I would rather live with a lion and a dragon"). The patriarchal assumptions include shame over living off the wife's money (25:22), the idea that woman is the origin of sin (25:24; see Gen 3:6, 12-13; 1 Tim 2:14), and the husband's prerogative in divorce (25:26; Deut 24:1-4; Mark 10:2-10; Matt 19:3-9). The contrasting section on the good wife (26:1-4) uses the beatitude form ("Happy is the husband of a good wife") and portrays the good wife as the source of long life, joy, and peace for her husband. The second description of the evil wife (26:5-12) consists of a numerical proverb (25:5-6), three sayings on bad wives (25:7-9), and advice to the sage to keep strict sexual control over a rebellious daughter (25:10-12; see 42:9-14). The language ("tent peg . . . quiver") is very graphic. The contrasting section on the good wife (26:13-18) praises her virtues (charm, silence, modesty) and physical beauty. Though present only in some Greek manuscripts and in the Syriac version, 26:19-27 was very likely part of the original text. The ideal for the sage is to marry a wife from the daughters of Israel and to raise up many children from her (26:19-21).

The concluding contrasts between evil women and good women (26:22-27) help us to understand Ben Sira's ideal woman as pious, modest, honoring her husband, and quiet.

26:28–27:29: Sin and Related Topics. The eight short units in this section concern three depressing sights (26:28), business and temptation to sin (26:29–27:3), speech as a criterion of the person (27:4-7), pursuing justice and truth (27:8-10), the speech of the godly and the fool (27:11-15), betraying confidences as the death of friendship (27:16-21), the hypocrite (27:22-24), and retribution (27:25-29). These topics are treated often with colorful and memorable rhetorical devices: the numerical proverb culminating in grief over the righteous person turning back to sin (26:28), the image of sin wedged like a stake between selling and buying (27:2), some scatological images (27:4), the idea of "doing the truth" (27:9), checking the time with fools but lingering with the wise (27:12), the inclusion about one who betrays confidences losing hope (27:16, 21), the vehement hatred for the hypocrite (27:24), and the comical images of retribution—how people destroy themselves with their own evil devices (27:25-29).

27:30–28:7: Forgiveness of Sins. Two basic attributes of God in the Bible are justice and mercy. Those who seek vengeance from others (27:30–28:1) will have to face the justice of God. Those who seek God's mercy must be willing to show mercy to others (28:2-5)—a point made in five slightly different ways. As further motivation for forgiveness, the sage is urged to "remember" death and the commandments of God's covenant (28:6-7). Only those who deal mercifully with others can expect mercy from God. Otherwise they should prepare for strict justice from God.

28:8-26: Destructive Speech. The four sections approach destructive speech from various perspectives. The root of strife, discord, and bloodshed (28:8-12) is the mouth, which can either ignite the flame or put it out (28:12). The unit on slander (28:13-16) focuses on its effects in destroying peace (28:13, 16) and in ruining men (28:14) and women (28:15), who are then driven from their homes (by divorce) and left without means. The destructive power of the tongue (28:17-23) is illustrated by a series of comparisons: worse than the whip, sword, yoke and fetters, death and Hades (= Sheol), flames, and lion and leopard. The final section (28:24-26) is direct advice to the wise about the value of being cautious in speech with the aid of various images: fence of thorns, door and bolt, lock, balances and scales, and the prospect of ambush (see Jas 3:1-12).

29:1-20: Money Matters. The section on loans (29:1-7) first states general principles: Be willing to make loans as the Torah dictates (Exod

22:25; Lev 25:35-37; Deut 15:7-11; 23:19-20; 24:10-13) without taking interest from a fellow Israelite, and be scrupulous in paying back what you have borrowed. Then it reflects on the dangers of making loans in 29:4-7: You may not get paid back and may make an enemy for your trouble. The section on almsgiving (29:8-13) assumes that this is a good deed in accord with the Torah (see Deut 15:7) and focuses on the positive effects that are sure to come from such generosity with the image of a "treasure." Though Proverbs recommends against providing surety or collateral for another (see Prov 6:1-5; 11:15; 17:18; 20:16; 22:26-27; 27:13), Ben Sira in 29:14-20 is favorably disposed toward the practice ("a good person will be surety for his neighbor") but also aware of the dangers and negative effects. His basic principle in standing surety and in all these money matters is expressed in 29:20: "Assist your neighbor to the best of your ability, but be careful not to fall yourself."

29:21-28: Depending on Others. The situation presupposed by the instruction is sketched in Lev 25:35: "If any of your kin fall into difficulty and become dependent on you, you shall support them; they shall live with you as though resident aliens." Whereas the Torah looks at the situation from the side of the dispenser of charity, Ben Sira views it from the perspective of the recipient. In 29:21-22 he counts having one's own home among the necessities of life, however humble that home may be. That modicum of independence contrasts with the shame of depending on the kindness of others who may treat you like a servant (29:25-26) and throw you out (29:27). The concluding comment about "the insults of the money-lender" (29:28) may allude to the cause of the dependency and so relate the passage to what preceded it.

30:1-13: Fathers and Sons. A father should discipline his son because it will benefit the son in the long run and increase the father's reputation before others. Ben Sira's theories about raising children sound very dubious today, but they were hardly unique in antiquity (see Prov 13:24; 19:18; 22:15; 23:13-14). The first section (30:1-6) reflects on the positive effects of disciplining the son, and the second section (30:7-12) considers the negative effects of forgoing discipline. The final verse (30:13) summarizes the teaching: "Discipline your son and make his yoke heavy, so that you may not be offended by his shamelessness." The cultural ideal of the father is that he should be stern, distant (see 30:9-10), and deserving of respect.

30:14-25: Happiness. Three important elements in happiness are good physical health (30:14-17), good food (30:18-20), and a good disposition (30:21-25). Whereas good health is more valuable than gold or silver, death is preferable to bad health. The section on food (30:18-20) is somewhat obscure in its imagery. The idea seems to be that for one who is sick and unable to eat (understood as a punishment from God; see 30:19), good food is as useless as what is set out by a grave or sacrificed to an idol and as fruitless as a girl embraced by a eunuch. The positive effects of a good disposition include a long life (30:22) and good digestion (30:25).

31:1-11: Riches. Does wealth bring happiness and righteousness? The question is answered negatively in four small units. The first (31:1-2) establishes that concern over money is a major cause of sleeplessness. The second (31:3-4) contrasts the leisure of the rich and the life of the poor. For the poor to take time off only increases their need. Far from bringing about righteousness, the pursuit of riches leads to ruin and destruction (31:5-7). The final unit (31:8-11) is a beatitude that praises the rich person who is blameless and not greedy. The Hebrew text of 31:8 uses the term "Mammon" (see Luke 16:9, 13) for wealth.

31:12–32:13: Manners and Moderation. How should one behave when invited to a banquet? The four units form a chiastic structure: table manners (31:12-18); moderation with food (31:19-24); moderation with wine (31:25-31); table manners (32:1-13). All four units assume an "upper-class" culture in which public behavior is important in establishing and maintaining status. The first instruction on table manners (31:12-18) is a list of "dos" and "don'ts" to be observed when seated at the banquet table. The goal is to avoid drawing negative attention to oneself. The positive criterion ("judge your neighbor's feelings by your own") is a version of the New Testament Golden Rule (Matt 7:12; Luke 6:31). The first instruction about moderation (31:19-24) compares the results of moderate and immoderate eating and proposes the rule: "In everything you do be moderate, and no sickness will overtake you" (31:22). The last two verses (31:23-24) take up a different but loosely related topic by contrasting public responses to generous and stingy hosts. The second instruction on moderation compares the bad effects of drinking too much wine (31:25-26, 29-30) with the good effects of the moderate use of wine (31:27-28). The unit ends by advising the sage not to try to reason with a drunk (31:31). The final instruction on manners (32:1-13) first (32:1-2) counsels one who has been chosen to serve as "master of the feast" to do his duty in an inconspicuous manner—which ironically will increase his good reputation. The elder (32:3-6) is urged to speak in a restrained and accurate way and warned not to interfere with the precious musical entertainment. The younger man (32:7-10) is also urged to speak sparingly but at the same time to maintain modesty and diffidence— the kind of behavior that wins general approval. The unit ends in 32:11-13 with advice on going home in good time and on saying "grace" after the meal ("above all bless your Maker, who fills you with his good gifts").

32:14–33:6: Wisdom, Torah, and Fear of the Lord. Ben Sira's ideal sage combines practical wisdom, keeping the commandments, and fear of the Lord. The individual sections in this unit reflect on the relation of the three entities in various ways. The term "law" here refers specifically to the divine law revealed to Israel as the pattern for its relationship with God (the Torah). The first section (32:14-17) contrasts the sage who seeks the Law and fears God with the hypocrite and sinner who avoid correction and the statutes of the Law. The second section (32:18-24) begins as a mere call to cautious behavior, but then links such behavior to "the keeping of the commandments" and to fear of the Lord. The third section (33:1-3) again links wisdom, the Law, and fear of the Lord, and promises happiness and safety to those who act according to them. The final section (33:4-6) contrasts the thoughtful preparation of the wise before speaking with the mindless behavior of the fool. This text (with other such passages) goes to the heart of Ben Sira's intellectual program of fusing the common Near Eastern wisdom tradition with the distinctively Jewish experience of God and approach to life.

33:7-15: The Pairs. Throughout his work Ben Sira has distinguished sages and fools, good and bad, life and death, without ever explaining how an all-good and all-powerful God could allow the existence of evil (the question of theodicy). Finally he approaches this issue with his doctrine of the "pairs," which is articulated most clearly in 33:14-15: Within God's plan for creation there is a certain dualism (good versus evil, life versus death, godly versus sinners). Ben Sira leads up to this teaching by reflecting on the Jewish calendar (33:7-9), in which some days are important (Passover, Sabbaths, etc.) and other days get only a number (day one, day two, etc.). Then he applies this duality to God's creation of human beings (33:10-13) and dealings with them ("like clay in the hand of the potter"). Ben Sira proposes a modified dualism in which everything (good and evil) remains under God's sovereignty (see Isa 45:7) and appeals somewhat vaguely to the divine plan working itself out in the "nature of things." He does not present a strong Satan figure who leads the children of darkness to do the deeds of darkness.

33:16-19: Autobiographical Note. Unlike most biblical books, Sirach is neither anonymous nor pseudonymous. The author identifies himself by name (50:27) and sprinkles his book with autobiographical comments (24:30-34; 33:16-19; 34:9-13; 39:12-13; 50:27; 51:13-30). By comparing himself first to a gleaner and then to a skilled grape picker he suggests that his long study and appropriation of the biblical and wisdom traditions have yielded rich results (33:16-17). Then he affirms that his study and teaching are not for himself, but rather for the general public (33:18-19). The wisdom teacher has a public vocation and benefits others.

33:20-33: Master of the Household. Ben Sira addresses the head of the household, who is assumed to be a male and to have financial resources and slaves. He first (33:20-24) urges the householder to preserve his independence ("do not let anyone take your place") and not to distribute his property until the hour of death. In Ben Sira's day human slavery was an economically, socially, and even religiously sanctioned institution. Persons became slaves by being taken captive in war or by financial reverses. Ben Sira's initial advice (33:25-30a), however pragmatic and effective, is very harsh ("bread and discipline and work for a slave"); it is tempered somewhat by an appeal for justice in 33:30b. The advice ends (33:31-33) with the case of a householder who has only one slave and whose self-interest demands good treatment of the slave.

34:1-20: Sources of Wisdom and Happiness. The first section (34:1-8) is strong critique of the value of dreams. In antiquity dreams were thought to give knowledge about the future (unlike the modern psychoanalytic use of dreams as indicators of the past). With sharp insight Ben Sira calls dreams a mere reflection of the self (34:3). He makes an exception for dreams "sent by invention from the Most High" (34:6; see Gen 28:12-16; 31:10-13, 24; 37:5-10; 40:8-19; 41:1-32; Dan 2:1-19, 27-45; Matthew 1–2). But how does one know? Instead of relying on dreams, it is preferable to fulfill the Law and thus exercise perfect wisdom. The second section (34:9-13) praises the value of experience gained through travel and includes Ben Sira's autobiographical testimony (34:12-13; see 33:16-19) about how experience saved him from the dangers of travel (see 2 Cor 11:25-27). The third section (34:14-20) reflects on the positive ideal of fear of the Lord: "Happy is the soul who fears the Lord." With a series of striking images ("a shelter from scorching wind and a shade from noonday sun . . . he lifts up the soul and makes the eyes sparkle") Ben Sira describes the blessings that accompany one who fears the Lord, which is true wisdom.

34:21–35:26: True Religion and Social Justice. The three sections in this unit are reminiscent of the language and ideas of Isaiah 56–66. Ben Sira, who was positively disposed toward and even enthusiastic for Temple worship (see 50:1-21), insists that religious practices be accompanied and animated by a concern for social justice. The first section (34:21-31) makes that point in a series of short units (vv. 21-23, 24-27, 28-29, 30-31). God will not accept the sacrifices of those who have exploited the poor (see Jas 5:16). The most striking images appear in 34:30-31, which alludes to the fast of the Day of Atonement (see Lev 23:27-32). Unless the fast is accompanied by a resolve not to sin again, God will not hear prayers for forgiveness of sins. Such presumption is compared to someone who incurs ritual defilement by touching a corpse (see Num 19:11-13), goes through the process of ritual cleansing, and touches the corpse again. The second section (35:1-13) begins with a short poem (35:1-5) that equates observing the commandments, doing acts of kindness, and avoiding sin with various elements in the Temple cult (see Isaiah 58). Yet good deeds do not substitute for Temple worship, nor do they stand in opposition to it. The second poem (35:6-13) is an enthusiastic endorsement of offering sacrifices at the Temple during the pilgrimage festivals ("Do not appear before the Lord empty-handed") and a plea for generosity in offering first fruits and tithes ("With every gift show a cheerful face"). The theological dynamic of sacrifice is *do ut des* ("I give that you may give") on the assumption that God "will repay you sevenfold" (35:13). The third section (35:14-26) focuses on the justice of God. As the just judge, God cannot be bribed by dishonest sacrifices (35:14-15). God will attend to the complaints of orphans and widows (35:16-19) and to the prayers of humble and righteous people (35:20-22a, "the prayer of the humble pierces the clouds"). The concluding description of God as a delivering warrior (35:22b-26) features four "until" clauses and ends with a beautiful image of God's mercy being as welcome "as clouds of rain in time of drought." The language of 35:22b-26 is reminiscent of the prophets and very much at home in Jewish apocalypticism with its themes of the destruction of the unrighteous, judgment according to deeds, and vindication and happiness for God's faithful people.

36:1-22: Prayer for God's People. This lament urging God's intervention on Israel's behalf follows from the description of the Lord as warrior in 35:22b-25. The first part (36:1-12) addresses the "God of all" and contrasts "no God but you" (36:5) with enemy rulers who say "There is no one but ourselves" (36:12). Though Ben Sira may have had in mind the Seleucid king Antiochus III, the language is so biblical and traditional that one cannot identify a specific figure or occasion. His appeal is expressed in the language associated with the Exodus ("new signs . . . other wonders . . . make your hand and right arm glorious"). What is at stake is not so much Israel's reputation, but God's reputation: "As you have used us to show your holiness to them, so use them to show your glory to us" (36:4). Whereas the first part urges God's intervention against the Gentiles, the second part (36:13-22) prays for the ingathering of all Israel and God's blessing on the Jerusalem Temple. Again (as is frequent in the Psalms), the appeal is to God's own self-interest: God's people and his Temple should be glorious; God's prophecies should be fulfilled; and all peoples should know "that you are the Lord, the God of the ages" (36:22).

36:23–37:15: Friends and Associates. The three main instructions are prefaced by a short unit on discernment or discretion (36:23-25) that evokes by way of comparison the ability of the tongue and stomach to tell one food from another. The section on choosing a wife (36:26-31) compares the happiness of a man married to a beautiful and modest woman (36:27-29) with the rootlessness and aimlessness of the unmarried man (36:30-31; see Gen 4:12, 14). Ben Sira's cultural assumptions come out in his comment that "a woman will accept any man as a husband" (marriages were arranged, and the woman had no choice), and in his remark that he who acquires a wife gets "his best possession." In choosing a friend (37:1-6) one should beware of "friends only in name," friends who become enemies, and "fair weather" friends (37:1, 2, 4). Failures in friendship are traced to the "inclination to evil" (37:3), an important concept in Ben Sira's approach to the human condition. But friends who prove faithful in times of testing ("during the battle") should be rewarded (37:5-6). In choosing a counselor (37:7-15) one should find out the counselor's own agenda and interests, lest the counselor work only to his own advantage (37:7-9). This basic principle is followed by a list of inappropriate counselors (37:10-11), including a woman about her rival (as a second wife?) and a lazy servant about a big task. The best sources of good advice (37:12-15) are those who keep the commandments, one's own heart and mind, and God in prayer.

37:16-31: Wisdom and Moderation. The first unit (37:16-18) explores the relation between words, plans, and actions (and their results). It calls the word "the beginning of every work" and the tongue a ruler. The second unit (37:19-26) contrasts clever people who lack wisdom (37:19-21) and the truly wise person who benefits both himself and his people (37:22-26). The several references to the "people" may account for the saying about the days of Israel being "without number" (37:25). Moderation in eating (37:27-31; see 31:19-31) is characteristic of a wise person. One must approach food with discretion and restraint lest one grow sick and die (see Num 11:18-20). The references to sickness prepare for the advice about physicians that follows.

38:1-15: Sickness and Doctors. The sage is urged first to be respectful and cooperative with physicians (38:1-3) and to look upon medicines as gifts from God (38:4-8). Ben Sira emphasizes that both physicians and medicines have been created by God and work their healing as instruments of God. The allusion in "water made sweet with a tree" (38:5) is to the Marah incident in Exod 15:23-25. The sage, when sick, is instructed first to attend to the spiritual duties of prayer, repentance, and sacrifice (38:9-11), and then to cooperate fully with the physician (38:12-15). Again there is an emphasis on God's action: Physicians too should pray that they may make the correct diagnosis and be successful in healing (38:14). This ideal situation contrasts with that of King Asa (2 Chr 16:12) who did not seek the Lord but sought help only from physicians (38:15). In this advice Ben Sira blends reliance both on God and on doctors and their medicines.

38:16-23: Mourning. When a loved one dies, grief should be intense but circumscribed. The first section (38:16-17) describes the rituals associated with mourning and urges serious compliance with them "for one day, or two." But Ben Sira is more concerned with the harmful effects of excessive grief (38:18-20) and concludes with a meditation on the inevitability and finality of death (38:21-23). Though there is no explicit denial of life after death, neither is there much affirmation of it ("the dead is at rest"). Ben Sira's real interest is in facing the fact of physical death and its value in placing grief over the death of a loved one in proper perspective.

38:24–39:11: Tradesmen and the Scribe. For Ben Sira scribes were far more than those who copied documents. They not only could read and write but also were public figures, intellectuals, and rightful leaders. Such persons were trained at Ben Sira's school (see 51:23-28). The first part (38:24-34a) contrasts the leisure of the scribe (38:24) with the preoccupations of the farmer (38:25-26), artisan (38:27), smith (38:28), and potter (38:29-30). The scribe has the "leisure" (Greek *scholē*, from which derive "school," "scholar," "scholastic," etc.) that befits the "free" person (Latin *liber,* from which derives our idea of a "liberal" education), and so has the opportunity to learn and develop the necessary intellectual and rhetorical skills. The passage is often compared to the Egyptian satire on the trades (in "The Instruction of Khety, Son of Duauf"). Ben Sira, far from denigrating tradesmen (see 38:31-32a, 34a), acknowledges their positive and necessary contributions to society. Yet they cannot do what the scribe does: exercise political and legal leadership (38:32b-33). Ben Sira's description of the scribal ideal first lists the components of a proper scribal education (38:34b-39:4), which includes the Law of the Most High and other elements of Israel's religious tradition, the ancient wisdom collections (proverbs and parables), service among the great, and travel (see 34:9-13). This learning must be accompanied by prayer and the wisdom of the Torah, because

God is the ultimate source of wisdom (39:5-8). The reward of such scribal discipline is public recognition and fame, as well as a "name" that lives on after the scribe's death (39:9-11). Immortality through memory is the fitting tribute to the faithful scribe.

39:12-35: God's Creation and Evil. The most difficult question facing any scribe (or philosopher or theologian) is the problem of evil. After a call to listen and to praise God (39:12-15), Ben Sira affirms the goodness of creation and the absolute sovereignty of God over it (39:16-21). With an allusion to Gen 1:9-10 ("at his word the waters stood in a heap"), Ben Sira places special emphasis on God's purpose in creation ("everything has been created for its own purpose"). The author's solution to the dilemma (39:22-31) affirms that God created good things for good people, but for evil people these can become bad (39:25). Thus the ten necessities of human life ("water and fire and iron and salt . . ." 39:26) can turn into evil for sinners. And things that have bad effects ("winds . . . fire and hail and famine and pestilence," 39:28-30) can serve to punish the wicked. While preserving the sovereignty of God and tracing evil to the perverted will of the wicked, Ben Sira leaves untouched the problem of innocent suffering explored in Job. In his epilogue (39:32-35) Ben Sira reaffirms that "all the works of the Lord are good" and "everything proves good in its appointed time." See his earlier reflection on "the pairs" in 33:7-15.

40:1-30: Misery and Joy. These topics are treated in four loosely connected units on the misery associated with the human condition (40:1-10), the triumph of righteousness (40:11-17), the joys of life (40:18-27), and the misery of begging (40:28-30). The first unit (40:1-10) traces the fears and anxieties all humans face to the "heavy yoke . . . laid on the children of Adam," which is surely a reference to Genesis 3 but probably not yet a doctrine of "original sin" as in Romans 5. The description of restless sleep and bad dreams in 40:5b-7 is especially vivid and true to life. The issue of innocent suffering is broached in 40:8-10, where all are said to share in the punishments intended for the wicked (who suffer sevenfold). These somber thoughts are balanced by a confidence (40:11-17) that wickedness and the wicked will be swept away and what will abide are good faith, kindness, and almsgiving. Though Ben Sira probably expected this triumph within the normal course of history, the content fits well with the apocalyptic language of Daniel and some New Testament passages. The third unit (40:18-27) is a numerical proverb of an unusual kind. Each of the ten sections (nine in Greek) names two good things and asserts that a third thing is even better. Thus wealth and a salary are good, but finding a treasure is even better. The list climaxes in the declaration that fear of the Lord is best of all (40:26-27).

The worst misery that befalls human beings is to be reduced to begging (40:28-30): "It is better to die than to beg." Again Ben Sira shows keen psychological insight by calling attention to the loss of self-respect and the internal hostility that accompany begging.

41:1-13: Death and Reputation. An important mode of immortality is the "name"—the reputation and memory one leaves behind. The opening reflection on death (41:1-4) provides the framework for what follows: Death is unwelcome to the prosperous and welcome to the wretched; it is nonetheless "the Lord's decree for all flesh" and so inevitable. Through their "abominable children" (41:5-10) sinners suffer perpetual disgrace, for their children not only endure the disgrace of their parents but also replicate their behavior. This bleak picture is punctuated by a warning: "Woe to you, the ungodly, who have forsaken the Law of the Most High" (41:8). This helps to define the sinful behavior Ben Sira had in mind. The positive side (41:11-13) is developed in three verses about how a good and virtuous "name" lives forever. This teaching prepares for the catalogue of Israel's heroes in Sirach 44–50.

41:14–42:8: Shame. After a brief comment on the public character of wisdom (41:14-15 = 20:30-31), Ben Sira distinguishes things of which one should and should not be ashamed (41:16). The list of shameful things (41:17–42:1a) includes both actions that bring shame and persons before whom one would be ashamed to do them. The first and most important thing in the list of things not to be ashamed of (42:1b-8) is "the Law of the Most High and his covenant" (42:2). The two lists provide interesting mixes of actions and persons. Knowing how to discern between what does and does not bring shame leads to a good "name" for the sage (42:1a, 8).

42:9-14: Fathers and Daughters. As was the case in the advice about disciplining one's son (30:1-13), the major concern is the father's reputation before others. The assumption is that daughters in "good" families will live protected lives as they are prepared for arranged marriages. The passage consists of a list of a father's worries about his daughter (42:9-10) and a stern warning to supervise her closely (42:11-13). If not, the father runs the risk of becoming a public "laughingstock." The low point in Ben Sira's misogynism comes in 42:14a: "Better is the wickedness of a man than a woman who does good."

42:15–43:33: God's Glory in Creation. Ben Sira's understanding of wisdom (fear of the Lord and keeping the commandments) takes as its horizon or background the glory of God made manifest in creation (42:15–43:33) and in Israel's history (44:1–50:24). At this point the book puts aside the practical advice so characteristic of the wisdom movement and offers a historical and theological framework in which the practical advice gains meaning and depth. The introductory poem (42:15-25) praises God's creation as "full of his glory" and reflects on the omniscience of God and God's purpose in creation. That all creation is made "by the word of the Lord" (42:15) recalls Genesis 1 but also alludes to the praise of Wisdom in Sirach 24 and forward to 43:26 ("by his word all things hold together"). Ben Sira also reasserts his modified dualism in 42:24 ("all things come in pairs"); see 33:7-15; 39:12-35; 40:8-10. The second poem (43:1-12) celebrates God's glory made manifest in heavenly bodies: sun (43:2-5), moon (43:6-8), stars (43:9-10), and rainbow (43:11-12). It gives special attention to the moon's role in fixing Israel's calendar ("the sign for festal days"), thus suggesting the use of a lunar calendar at the Jerusalem Temple. (Others followed a solar calendar.) For the rainbow in the Noah story see Gen 9:12-17. The third section (43:13-26) echoes the ancient "storm" poem in Psalm 29 and celebrates God's glory in the elements of nature: snow, lightning, clouds, hailstones, and so on. The imagery is quite striking and violent, but the assumption is that everything in nature fulfills God's purpose (see 43:26). Compare the climactic poem in Job 38–39, where the emphasis is on the human inability to grasp God's purpose. The fourth section (43:27-33) proclaims that God is "the all"—not in a pantheistic sense but rather in the biblical sense of Creator and Lord. The proper response to the manifestation of God's glory in nature is praise: "you cannot praise him enough" (43:30). The final verses (43:32-33) acknowledge the limits of human understanding ("I have seen but a few of his works"; see 42:15) and affirm that God is the source of wisdom for persons of piety.

44:1-15: God's Glory in Israel. How God's glory has been made manifest in Israel's history (see Wisdom 10–19) is the theme of chapters 44–50 ("Now let us praise famous men"). Ben Sira presents these great figures of Israel's past as manifestations of God's glory. The introductory poem (44:1-15) makes this point in the invocation (44:1-2): "The Lord apportioned to them great glory." The reflection is introduced by a list of twelve types of famous men (44:3-6). The persons celebrated in these chapters deserve the immortality by name and memory so praised by Ben Sira in 41:11-13. How 44:9 fits in the context of 44:7-15 is debated. It can be taken as a simple acknowledgment that some people are forgotten. Or it can more likely refer to oblivion as the fate of the wicked (see 41:5-10). For similar catalogues of Israel's heroes see 1 Macc 2:51-64 and Hebrews 11. The climax of Ben Sira's catalogue is Simon the high priest around 200 B.C.E. (see 50:1-24). These seven chapters can be regarded as preparation for the encomium of Simon. Much of what Ben Sira chooses to emphasize (glory, covenant, priesthood, Temple, building projects, etc.) has been chosen to lead up to his portrait of Simon.

44:16-23: The Patriarchs. Because of his mysterious transfer to heaven (Gen 5:24), Enoch (44:16) evoked great interest as a revealer of heavenly secrets and thus was a fitting character to begin and end (49:14) the list of heroes. Why he was hailed as an "example of repentance" is not clear (see Wis 4:10-12). Noah (44:17-18) is described as "perfect" (Gen 6:9) and "righteous" (Gen 7:1), and as the vehicle for "everlasting covenants" (Gen 9:8-17). Abraham (44:19-21) is the "great father of a multitude of nations" (Gen 17:4-5). What Ben Sira regarded as most important about Abraham is that "he kept the Law of the Most High" (long before the Law was given to Moses on Sinai!) and that he entered into the covenant of circumcision (see Genesis 17). Thus Abraham's fatherhood of many nations is through the distinctive elements of Israel's tradition: the Law and circumcision. God's promise to Abraham is carried on through Isaac (44:22a), and Jacob and his twelve sons (44:22b-23).

45:1-26: Moses, Aaron, and Phinehas. With the short but enthusiastic description of Moses (45:1-5) as a miracle worker and teacher, Ben Sira continues his motif of God's glory (45:2, 3) by allusions to Exodus 33–34. As the one to whom God revealed the commandments (45:3, 5), Moses was empowered to "teach Jacob the covenant" (45:5)—an important link between the covenant and the Torah in the unfolding of Israel's history. The disproportionately large space given to Aaron (45:6-22) prepares for the climax of chapters 44–50 with the praise of Simon in 50:1-24. God made an "everlasting covenant" with Aaron (45:7) and "added glory" to him (45:20). The detailed descriptions of the high priest's vestments in 45:8-13 (based on Exodus 28 and 39) and his functions of offering sacrifice and rendering judgments for the people in 45:14-17 foreshadow the description of Simon in 50:5-21. The episode of Korah, Dathan, and Abiram (Numbers 16) illustrates God's protection of Aaron (45:18-19), which is indicative of the special status of the priesthood (45:20-22; see Num 18:20; Deut 12:12). The section on Aaron's grandson Phinehas (45:23-26; see Num 25:7-13) carries on the motifs of glory (45:23, 26) and covenant (45:24, 25), and reinforces the importance of the priesthood with a short prayer (45:26).

46:1-20: Joshua and Caleb, the Judges, and Samuel. Joshua and Caleb (46:1-10) move forward the history of the covenant by defeating Israel's enemies and leading Israel into "the land flowing with milk and honey."

For Joshua's military exploits see Joshua 1–11; and for the mission of Joshua and Caleb see Num 14:6-10 and Josh 14:6-11. Ben Sira suggests that God used them to teach lessons to the Gentiles ("he was fighting in the sight of the Lord," 46:6) and to Israel ("how good it is to follow the Lord," 46:10). Only those judges (46:11-12) who did not fall into idolatry (compare Gideon in Judg 8:22-35) are blessed; for bones sending forth life see 2 Kgs 13:21. The primary role attributed to Samuel (46:13-20) is prophet. But he is also a judge (46:14) and a priest (46:16; see 1 Sam 7:9). As the prophet of the Lord, Samuel functioned as a kind of "elder statesman" who established the monarchy and anointed Saul and David as kings. His integrity was beyond doubt (46:19; see 1 Sam 12:1-5), and even after death he prophesied on Israel's behalf (46:20; see 1 Samuel 28).

47:1-25: Early Kings. Nathan (47:1; see 2 Samuel 7 and 12) provides continuity with Samuel the prophet in the time of David. The treatment of David (47:2-11) highlights his election by God (47:2-3), his exploits as a warrior (47:4-7), and his initiatives in public worship at Jerusalem (47:8-10). The motif of glory is again prominent (47:6 [twice], 8, 11), and the references to worship prepare for the description of Simon in 50:5-21. The summary evaluation (47:11) presents David as a forgiven sinner to whom God gave "a covenant of kingship and a glorious throne in Israel." Solomon (47:12-22) was chosen by God to reign in a time of peace and to build the Jerusalem Temple where Simon would preside some eight hundred years later (47:12-13). Using the device of direct address, Ben Sira divides his treatment of Solomon into a celebration of his wisdom (47:14-17) and a somber reflection on his greed and lust (see Deut 17:17) that resulted in division between Israel and Judah (47:18-21). Solomon stained his own "glory/honor" and made himself an example of folly (47:20). Yet the covenant with David continued (47:22) despite the split caused by Rehoboam and Jeroboam (47:23; see 1 Kings 12) and the subsequent history of sin and exile (47:24-25). The affirmation of God's fidelity to the covenant with David is a rare "messianic" passage in Sirach and is especially poignant in the context of sin and exile.

48:1–49:16: Prophets and Kings. Ben Sira gives a fairly full summary of the exploits of Elijah the great prophet of the northern kingdom of Israel (48:1-11; see 1 Kings 17–19 and 2 Kings 1–2), and a shorter summary about Elisha (48:12-14; see 2 Kings 2–13). Both stood up to wicked kings (48:6, 8, 12). With regard to Elijah, Ben Sira again uses the device of direct address in 48:4-11 ("How glorious you were, Elijah, in your wondrous deeds!"). He also alludes to the prophecy of Elijah's return (48:10; see Malachi 3–4), which is prominent in the New Testament. He gives disproportionate attention to the lifegiving power of Elisha's bones (48:13-14; see also 46:12 and 49:10). Yet, according to 48:15a, the prophets could not overcome the people's sinfulness, which led to the defeat and exile of Israel in 722 B.C.E. The fortunes of the southern kingdom of Judah are described with reference to its prophets and kings (48:15b–49:13). The only good kings of Judah (as in 1–2 Kings) were Hezekiah (48:17-22) and Josiah (49:1-3). Ben Sira praises Hezekiah's building projects (48:17; see 50:1-4 for Simon's building projects) and his leadership with Isaiah's help during the invasion by Sennacherib (48:18-21; see 2 Kings 18–19; Isaiah 36–37; 2 Chronicles 32). Isaiah (48:22-25) advised Hezekiah and even prolonged his life (see 2 Kgs 20:8-11; Isa 38:7-8). The references to Isaiah's comforting "the mourners in Zion" and revealing "what was to occur to the end of time" (48:24-25) indicate that Ben Sira regarded the entire book of Isaiah as coming from the pre-exilic prophet. The name of Josiah (49:1-3; see 2 Kings 22–23) is honored because he removed "the wicked abominations," whereas through the wickedness of the other kings of Judah (49:4-6) the "glory" of God's people was given over to a foreign nation despite the prophecies of Jeremiah (49:7; see Jer 1:10). Mention (49:8-10) is also made of Ezekiel ("who saw the vision of glory," see Ezekiel 1), Job (but the text is not certain), and the Twelve Prophets (see the "new life from the dead" motif also in 46:12; 48:14). As the catalogue moves toward Simon it praises the memories of Zerubbabel and Joshua (49:11-12; see Haggai) who rebuilt the Jerusalem Temple, and Nehemiah (49:13; see Neh 6:15) who rebuilt the city walls (see 50:14). The omission of Ezra is surprising. The final unit (49:14-16) moves backward to Adam by way of Enoch (see Gen 5:24), Joseph (see Gen 50:25-26; Exod 13:19), and Shem (Gen 11:10), and Seth (Gen 5:3-8). The high importance ascribed to Adam ("glorified above every living creature") is unparalleled in the Old Testament.

50:1-24: Simon the High Priest. The climactic figure in Ben Sira's parade of Israel's heroes is Simon (or Simeon) II, the son of Onias (Yohanan), who served as high priest from 219 to 196 B.C.E. He probably died a few years before Ben Sira wrote his book. The public works projects (50:1-4) that Simon organized served to strengthen the Temple and the city (as Solomon, Hezekiah, Zerubbabel and Joshua, and Nehemiah had done). A high point of the book is Ben Sira's description of Simon presiding at a Temple liturgy (either the Daily Offering or the Day of Atonement) in 50:5-21. Simon's entrance before the people is called "glorious" (50:5, 11), and the impression is heightened by a series of eleven similes in 50:6-10 ("like the morning star . . ."). Mention of the high priest's robe (a topic of great symbolic significance for Philo, Josephus, and the Church Fathers) reminds the reader of the elaborate description of Aaron's vestments (45:6-13). What follows is the order of the ritual: offering the parts of the sacrificial animals (50:12-14), pouring out wine as a libation (50:15), sounding of trumpets and prostration of the people (50:16-17), song and prayer (50:18-19), and the high priestly blessing (50:20-21; see Num 6:24-26). In response to this glorious scene Ben Sira calls Israel to bless the "God of all" and to ask for happiness, peace, mercy, and deliverance (50:22-24).

50:25-29: Postscript and Epilogue. The numerical proverb in 50:25-26 has no relation to what precedes or follows it; it sounds like a postscript or a stray note. The three hated nations—Seir (Edom or Idumea), Philistia (the "Sea Peoples" of old, perhaps the Greeks of Ben Sira's day), and Samaria—all had done great harm to Judah, at least in the eyes of Judeans like Ben Sira. The final unit (50:27-29) consists of a "signature" by the author and a beatitude on those who take his book seriously and act upon it. The work ends as it began, with a testimony to the importance of "fear of the Lord."

51:1-30: Three Appendixes. The first appendix (51:1-12) is a thanksgiving hymn embodying many of the conventions of the biblical genre and those in the Qumran Thanksgiving Hymns. Nothing in it demands that it was composed by Ben Sira. After the customary thanksgiving formula (51:1), it describes the many dangers (mostly slander and false accusation) from which the speaker has been rescued (51:2-6a) and how, in the extremity of danger, he turned to God in prayer (51:6b-10), and concludes with the customary formula of thanks (51:11-12) but without mention of offering sacrifices.

The second appendix (51:12ff.) is not part of the Greek or Syriac version but appears only in a medieval Hebrew manuscript. It is modeled on Psalm 136 ("for his mercy endures forever"). The epithets applied to God are mostly biblical phrases, and there are important parallels to the Jewish daily prayer known as the Eighteen Benedictions, especially regarding the messianic hopes and the patriarchs. Nothing in the text demands that Ben Sira was the author.

The third appendix (51:13-30) is an autobiographical poem on the search for wisdom. If Ben Sira did not write it, he should have, since its ideas and hopes capture the spirit of the whole book. Discovery of a large part of the Hebrew text in the Qumran Cave 11 Psalms Scroll indicates that it was originally an acrostic, each unit beginning with a new letter of the Hebrew alphabet. It first describes Ben Sira's search for and discovery of wisdom (51:13-17) and his effort at living by wisdom (51:18-22). The search involved prayer and Temple worship (51:13-14, 19) and ended with Ben Sira's praise of God (51:22). The second part of the poem (51:23-30) is Ben Sira's invitation for students to join his school. Though there is no set fee (51:25), this kind of schooling will result in acquiring silver and gold (51:28). Ben Sira's call to "put your neck under her yoke" (51:26; see 6:23-31) and his testimony "I have labored but little and found for myself much serenity" (51:27) are parallel to, if not the sources of, Jesus' invitation to discipleship in Matthew 11:28-30.

Conclusion

Reading the entire book of Sirach with this guide now puts the reader in a position to proceed to the next level in appreciating Ben Sira's achievements as a thinker, teacher, and writer, and to refer back conveniently as needed. This exposition has given particular attention to his literary skills, the social world in which he lived, and the message he wished to convey. In the chapters that follow the focus will be on how Ben Sira communicates his wisdom (form criticism), the assumptions that he made about life in his sociocultural world (social description), and his views on some key philosophical and theological matters in comparison with those of other ancient wisdom teachers (spiritual exercises). Meanwhile, the exposition given in this chapter can continue to serve as a reference resource as study of Ben Sira and his book continues.

CHAPTER FOUR

Ben Sira's Ways of Teaching

Ben Sira was a teacher. Before he was a teacher he actively sought wisdom for himself and made great progress in his search (51:17), presumably at some kind of wisdom school. Near the end of his book he issues an invitation to prospective students to come to his school: "Draw near to me, you who are uneducated, and lodge in my house of instruction" (51:23).

We do not have much solid information about schools in early-second-century B.C.E. Palestine.[1] In fact, the book of Sirach itself is one of the best sources for such information. For example, we do not really know if Ben Sira had his own school building, or how large his classes were, or whether he taught only on an individual tutorial basis ("my son"). We do know, however, that he trained young men to become "scribes." Scribal education certainly involved reading and writing, but those basic skills were most likely only admittance requirements at Ben Sira's school. According to 38:34b–39:5 the curriculum included "the study of the law of the Most High" as well as the wisdom of all the ancients, prophecies, the sayings of the famous, parables, and proverbs. This course of study looks like a "double major" in biblical studies and wisdom traditions.

While Ben Sira's students were surely literate, they lived in what was predominantly an oral and illiterate culture in which memory still played a very important role. We can suppose that Ben Sira's students were expected to commit much of his teaching to memory. Having all his wisdom at their recall would enable them to interpret situations and come up with the "right" saying in the concrete circumstances, thus adding to their reputation for wisdom.

---

[1] For what we know see Eric W. Heaton, *The School Tradition of the Old Testament* (New York: Oxford University Press, 1994).

The scribe's fondest hope was to gain a good reputation: "Nations will speak of his wisdom, and the congregation will proclaim his praise" (39:10).

To facilitate memorization by his students Ben Sira presented many of his teachings in small units such as two-member maxims or proverbs, prohibitions ("do not . . ."), short instructions on a topic ("my son . . ."), and so on. This is how ancient Near Eastern wisdom teachers traditionally taught. Ben Sira, however, greatly enlarged the repertoire of literary forms in a wisdom book by including prayers, hymns, and even the rewriting of biblical history. Analysis of the literary forms—the ways in which Ben Sira taught his students and still teaches his readers—is called "form criticism."[2]

In biblical studies the term "form criticism" refers to the various formal devices of communication used by the writers or their sources. In other words, it is the analysis of the literary forms in which they present their message. It is both a literary operation (isolating and describing the modes of communication) and (at least ideally) a historical operation (determining the form's setting in the life of a society or community). Form criticism asks two basic questions: What is the literary form of this text? and Does the literary form of this text tell us anything about the history of the community?

Every time we read a newspaper we practice form criticism. From our experience and education as readers we know from the external literary forms themselves the differences between a news report, an obituary, a book review, an editorial, and a baseball box score. Even before paying much attention to the content of the item, we already know something of what we can expect by way of information and (sometimes) have a sense of the social milieu it represents (professional sports, the mortuary, academia, etc.).

One of the most important developments in biblical studies in the twentieth century was the application of form criticism to the texts of the Bible. An especially valuable recognition was that the poems in what we call the book of Psalms follow certain literary scripts (laments, thanksgivings, hymns, etc.) and that most of them originated in connection with the worship services conducted at the Jerusalem Temple. In the study of the Psalms form criticism has proved its value as both a literary and a historical tool.

For other parts of the Hebrew Bible form criticism has at least helped us to appreciate better how the various biblical writers communicated. The

[2] The fundamental study of literary forms in Sirach remains Walter Baumgartner, "Die literarischen Gattungen in der Weisheit des Jesus Sirach," *ZAW* 34 (1914) 161–98. For more recent treatments see Patrick W. Skehan and Alexander A. Di Lella, *The Wisdom of Ben Sira.* AB 39 (Garden City, NY: Doubleday, 1987) 21–30; and James L. Crenshaw, "Sirach," in *New Interpreter's Bible* (Nashville: Abingdon, 1997) 5:613–20. See also Claus Westermann, *Roots of Wisdom: The Oldest Proverbs of Israel and Other Peoples* (Louisville: Westminster, 1994).

"historical books" (Genesis through 2 Kings) are full of narratives, that is, stories with characters and plots. The legal materials in the Torah feature apodictic or absolute statements ("You shall not kill") and casuistic or "case" statements (If/when the circumstances are such, then the penalty shall be this). The prophetic writings contain divine oracles ("Thus says the Lord"), reproaches, threats, and promises, as well as divine disputes, laments, exhortations, and narratives about symbolic actions.

In the wisdom books of the Bible the most basic literary form is the maxim or proverb: a brief statement expressing in a memorable way the results of human experience or observation. In accord with the conventions of biblical and ancient Near Eastern poetry, many proverbs consist of two parallel members. When the two members make the same point in similar ways it is called synonymous parallelism: "Whoever corrects a scoffer wins abuse; whoever rebukes the wicked gets hurt" (Prov 9:7). When the two members say opposite things it is called antithetical parallelism: "A scoffer who is rebuked will only hate you; the wise, when rebuked, will love you" (Prov 9:8). Other wisdom forms include the instruction, the comparison, the list, and the riddle. The wisdom teachings were expressed in ways that made their memorization easy, and many of them seem to have circulated in small units before being collected into the larger books like Proverbs and Sirach.

The principal settings in life proposed for wisdom teachings are the family ("my son") or clan, the royal court, and the school. In view of the breadth of the content and the international character of the wisdom movement it is difficult to settle on one of these life-settings as primary.

The book of Sirach, which is by far the largest ancient Jewish wisdom book extant, is an excellent vehicle for practicing form criticism. Ben Sira uses a wide array of modes of communication and provides many examples of the different literary forms employed in sapiential writings. And since Ben Sira seems to have conducted a school for prospective sages (see Sir 51:23-30), we can be sure of the life-setting of these literary forms (though some traditions he used may have had different origins). The more familiar we are with the literary media used by Ben Sira, the better we will come to understand and appreciate his teachings about living wisely.

Mashal

The most prominent literary form in ancient Jewish wisdom books and in Sirach in particular is often called the *mashal*. The word derives from a Hebrew root that means "be like, similar." The term refers to forms of comparative speech that draw analogies between two items. For example, in 3:30 Ben Sira says: "As water extinguishes a blazing fire, so almsgiving atones for sin." This simile calls upon an experience of everyday life to illustrate what Ben Sira regards as a spiritual truth.

The problem with using the term *mashal* is that it has a very wide range of meaning. It is not restricted to similes or metaphors. The Hebrew title of what is known in English as the book of Proverbs is *Mishle* (the construct plural of *mashal*). Most of us instinctively associate the title with the large and disparate collection of short two-member sayings ("proverbs" in the narrow sense) found in Proverbs 10–22. But, as we have seen, the biblical book of Proverbs also contains extended poems about seeking wisdom and avoiding folly in chapters 1–9, a substantial wisdom instruction in 22:17–24:22, various collections of other wisdom sayings, and a poetic description of the ideal wife in 31:10-31.

In practice the word *mashal* covers a multitude of literary forms, ranging from short comparisons (as in Sir 3:30) to the rather full narratives attributed to Jesus in the gospels ("parables"). Indeed, the word "parable" derives from the Greek verb *paraballō,* which means to put one thing beside another: "The kingdom of heaven is like . . . ." A parable is an example of comparative speech, and so its Hebrew equivalent is *mashal.*

In the biblical context a *mashal* or parable can be as simple as a one-sentence comparison (a simile or metaphor as in Sir 3:30) or as long and complex as Jesus' parable of the Prodigal Son in Luke 15:11-32. Since these terms are so elastic, it may be better to avoid the general terms and to look instead at the various categories of sapiential discourse and see how Ben Sira uses them and what he seeks to communicate through them.

Maxims/Proverbs

A maxim is a short statement of a truth based on experience, expressed in a memorable way and so furnishing a wise guide to live by. The book of Sirach is full of maxims. Whether they were already traditional (like our "a stitch in time saves nine" or "look before you leap") or formulated by Ben Sira himself is difficult to determine. But since Ben Sira presents himself as a font of traditional wisdom, determining his originality in this or that case need not be a major concern in our study of his book. Indeed, Ben Sira taught in a milieu in which handing on traditions was a highly respected activity, and no one held copyrights on the material. What counted for creativity was not total originality but rather transmitting the wisdom of the past with perhaps a little "tweaking." What mattered was the truth of the teaching, not the name of its creator.

Following the example of Proverbs and other ancient Near Eastern wisdom books, Ben Sira generally expresses his maxims in short two-member sayings. For example, in 3:31 he says: "Those who repay favors give thought to the future; when they fall, they will find support." Another example of a maxim appears in 6:5: "Pleasant speech multiplies friends, and a gracious tongue multiplies courtesies." The latter maxim serves as an introduction to the extended instruction about friendship in 6:5-17.

Whether Ben Sira created these maxims or simply handed them on, the point is that he presents them as wise teachings that distill a large amount of individual human observation and experience. Each maxim has two members and can be easily commited to memory. The maxims are entertaining and cause us to reflect on our own experience and ask whether what they say is true to our experience or not. If we affirm the truth of the maxim, then we can use it as a wise guide to the way we live.

What kinds of truth do these maxims communicate? They do not purport to carry the mathematical or logical authority of a scientific law, which by definition ought to be applicable in every case. Nor do they carry the persuasive authority that a philosophical or a legal argument might enjoy. Rather, they distill the witness (based on observation and experience) of someone (here Ben Sira) who claims that in most cases what the maxim says is true. However, these maxims generally concern the notoriously complex topics of human character, attitudes, and actions. And the kind of truth they carry may not hold in each particular case.

For example, is it really true that those who repay favors (see 3:31) can expect to be repaid in the future? It is doubtful, given Ben Sira's own skepticism about life after death and rewards from God at the final judgment, that he wants us to think of postmortem justice or vindication. Rather, it appears that by this maxim he wants us to consider our experiences—not only our personal experiences but also that of those around us—and to affirm the general truth of the maxim. As individuals we can probably ageee that in very many cases it is true that those who repay favors do find help from others when they are in need. But we may also think of cases where the maxim does not conform to our experience. In fact, there is the modern maxim according to which "no good deed goes unpunished." The opposing maxim fits those occasions when we have done a favor for someone but find ourselves criticized or greatly inconvenienced for our trouble, and not rewarded in any obvious way.

Again, is it true (with Sir 6:5) that pleasant speech really does multiply friends, and that a gracious tongue really does multiply courtesies? I can think of instances in which my attempts at politeness or good humor have been taken wrongly and met with rebuff or criticism. But in most cases in my experience it is true that polite and gracious speech is answered in kind. Moreover, such speech can open the way to friendships, which is the topic of what follows in 6:6-17. Having affirmed the basic truth of Sir 6:5, I can go through my day with its content as a guide to how I should meet and interact with other persons. However, I also recognize that there may be times when justice demands that I speak out forcefully and perhaps even impolitely.

The book of Sirach is full of maxims, and there is no point in attempting a truly comprehensive treatment of them all here. For now it is enough to recognize maxims for what they are: short statements of truth based on experience that are expressed in memorable ways and can serve as wise guides to live by. At the same time the maxims may also stimulate reflection on whether they prove true in actual situations.

Beatitudes

A common literary form in wisdom writings and in the Psalms is the beatitude, which is a short saying that declares someone "happy, fortunate, or blessed." It is as if you were to point to someone who appears to you to be especially fortunate and say, "Lucky him!" The keywords are *ashre* in Hebrew and *makarios* in Greek. Because of the Greek term the beatitudes are sometimes called "macarisms," since they proclaim someone to be *makarios*. They recognize the good fortune inherent in an action, attitude, or possession, and there is often the suggestion that this good fortune really comes from God. Their emphasis in Sirach and in the Hebrew Bible is on the past or present, as opposed to the New Testament beatitudes in Matt 5:3-12 and Luke 6:20-23, which look mainly to the eschatological future for their fulfillment in the kingdom of God.

In Sirach the beatitudes usually consist of two units, with the first unit beginning with *ashre* in Hebrew and *makarios* in Greek. The two units often give similar or parallel reasons why that person should be declared "happy" or "fortunate." The first two beatitudes in Sirach (14:1-2) form a pair: "Happy are those who do not blunder with their lips, and need not suffer remorse for sin. Happy are those whose hearts do not condemn them, and who have not given up their hope." The reader should note that in the effort at gender-inclusive language the *New Revised Standard Version* (and other recent translations) renders Ben Sira's masculine singular language of the beatitudes in Hebrew and Greek ("Happy is the man/he who . . .") in gender common plural language ("Happy are those who . . .").

Ben Sira uses beatitudes in various ways. Some (25:8; 26:19; 31:8; 34:17; 48:11) appear simply as part of a larger treatment of a theme. Others (14:1-2; 14:20; 26:1) introduce a unit. The final beatitude (50:28-29) is an apt summary of Ben Sira's teachings about wisdom and fear of the Lord, which are his two most important themes.

The beatitude in 14:20 ("happy is the person who meditates on wisdom") introduces one of the pivotal wisdom poems in Sirach, which reflects on the search for wisdom (14:20-27) and on the benefits of wisdom (15:1-10). In the numerical saying in 25:7-11 there are two beatitudes pronounced on "the man who lives with a sensible wife" and on "the one who does not sin with his tongue" (25:8). In 26:1-4 the section on the joy a good wife brings is introduced by a beatitude: "Happy is the husband of a good wife." And in the middle of a meditation on destructive speech (28:8-26) Ben Sira declares: "Happy is the one who is protected from it" (28:19).

The remaining beatitudes declare "happy" the rich person who is found blameless (31:8), the soul that fears the Lord (34:17), and those who saw Elijah with their own eyes (48:11). And in the epilogue of the book Ben Sira concludes the main text of his wise teachings (ch. 51 seems to be an appendix) with a beatitude that summarizes the work and states what he hopes that readers will learn from it: "Happy are those who concern themselves with these things, and those who lay them to heart will become wise. For if they put them into practice, they will be equal to anything, for the fear of the Lord is their path" (50:28-29).

Woes

In the Bible a "woe" saying is the opposite of a beatitude. For example, in Luke 6:20-26 four beatitudes (6:20-23) are paired with a corresponding set of four "woes" (6:24-26): "Blessed are you who are poor . . . Woe to you who are rich." The key words are *ʾoy* in Hebrew and *ouai* in Greek. In Sir 2:12-14 there is a set of three "woe" sayings in the midst of an instruction about fear of the Lord. These "woes" serve as warnings to or threats against those who may be timid or lazy (2:12), the fainthearted (2:13), and those who have lost their nerve (2:14). The remaining "woe" punctuates Ben Sira's reflection on death and reputation in 41:1-13: "Woe to you, the ungodly, who have forsaken the law of the Most High God!"

Numerical Sayings

Numerical sayings are common in ancient Near Eastern wisdom texts and appear also in Proverbs (see 6:16-19; 30:15b-16, 18-19, 21-23, 29-31). Most of the examples in Proverbs occur in the section designated as the "Words of Agur" (ch. 30). This literary form can be nicely illustrated by the numerical saying contained in Prov 30:18-19. There the saying is introduced by a number: "Three things are too wonderful for me." Then comes a parallel saying with that number plus one: "four I do not understand." And finally there is the list of items that "are too wonderful": "the way of an eagle in the sky, the way of snake on a rock, the way of a ship on the high seas, and the way of a man with a girl." The number in the introduction catches the attention of the hearer or reader. The suspense is heightened by the "number plus one" device, and the most important or interesting item generally appears at the end of the list.

Ben Sira uses numerical proverbs at several points near the center of his book (23:16-18; 25:1-2, 7-11; 26:5-6, 28) and once near the end (50:25-26). Whether Ben Sira himself coined these numerical proverbs or simply took them over from the wisdom tradition is not clear. What is distinctive is Ben Sira's strategy of using the numerical saying as the occasion for a further development of the last item on the list in the material that follows.

The numerical saying in 23:16-18 introduces a section on sins of the flesh (23:16-27). It begins with the number/number plus one formula: "Two kinds of individuals multiply sins, and a third incurs wrath." The list that follows concerns three kinds of sexual sins viewed from a male perspective: incest ("fornication with his next of kin"), fornication ("all bread is sweet"), and adultery ("one who sins against his marriage bed"). This numerical saying leads Ben Sira into a perceptive description of the adulterer's psychology in 23:18b-21. While the adulterer imagines that he will not get caught and thinks that God will not remember his sin, Ben Sira warns that the omniscient God does indeed notice and that eventually the adulterer's sin will be made public. The treatment of the (male) adulterer is followed by a discussion of the woman who bears a child to a man other than her husband (23:22-27). Ben Sira explains why such a woman should be regarded and punished as a sinner, and describes the consequences for her and her offspring. His only hope (23:27) is that the children born of such a union might eventually recognize the positive value of fear of the Lord and keeping God's commandments.

The two numerical sayings in Sirach 25 introduce (25:1-2) and conclude (25:7-11) a short section on happiness. The first numerical saying does not use the number/number plus one formula. Instead it presents two contrasting lists of three items each, one about pleasant things and the other about loathsome persons. The pleasant things (25:1) involve harmony among persons who are somehow close to one another: "agreement among brothers and sisters, friendship among neighbors, and a wife and a husband who live in happiness." The list of loathsome persons (25:2) includes "a pauper who boasts, a rich person who lies, and an old fool who commits adultery." These persons act in ways that are either unnecessary or inappropriate. The final item on the second list—the old fool who commits adultery—leads into a positive reflection on how attractive are sound judgment and wisdom in elderly persons (25:3-6).

The numerical saying in 25:7-11 that rounds off the section on happiness contains the longest list of items by far: "I can think of nine whom I would call blessed, and a tenth my tongue proclaims" (25:7a). At three points this list (25:8 [twice], 9) employs the "beatitude" formula: "Happy is . . . ." It includes people who can rejoice in their children, who live to see the downfall of their foes, and so forth. It culminates in declaring as truly happy "the one who finds wisdom . . . the one who fears the Lord" (25:10). Indeed, in Ben Sira's view, if one finds wisdom and fears the Lord one has found the basis of true happiness and all the other blessings will follow.

The fourth numerical saying (Sir 26:5-6) appears in the middle of a long section devoted to the bad wife and the good wife (25:13–26:27). There are alternating passages concerning bad wives (25:13-26; 26:5-12) and good wives (26:1-4; 26:13-18), along with advice about choosing a wife (26:19-21) and contrasts between the bad wife and the good wife (26:22-27). The numerical saying in 26:5-6 introduces the second passage about bad wives and proposes to list four frightening things: "Of three things . . . and of a fourth I am in great fear." The four frightening things are slander in the city, the gathering of a mob, false accusation, and "when a wife is jealous of a rival and tongue-lashing makes it known to all." The first three items have nothing to do with the section's general theme, but the fourth item explains why the numerical proverb appears where it does. We may assume that the wife is jealous of another woman. But whether her "rival" is a mistress, slave, or even a second wife is not clear. For the husband the real problem comes when the wife complains about "the other woman" in public and so brings embarrassment and shame on the husband and causes him to "lose face" among his peers.

The fifth numerical saying in 26:28 introduces a section (26:28–27:29) of short units dealing with sin and related topics. This saying concerns three ("at two things . . . because of a third") depressing sights. The depressing sights are "a warrior in want through poverty, intelligent men who are treated contemptuously, and a man who turns back from righteousness to sin." In this context again the most important item is the final one, which sets the tone and theme for what follows.

The final numerical saying in Sirach (50:25-26) is peculiar in its context and content. It appears immediately after Ben Sira's beautiful and uplifting description of Simon the high priest presiding at a liturgy in the Jerusalem Temple (50:1-24) and just before the epilogue in which Ben Sira identifies himself by name and declares "happy" those who take his teachings seriously and put them into practice (50:27-29). In form it is like the other numerical sayings: "Two nations my soul detests, and a third is not even a people" (50:26). But the content does not concern typical persons or events as the others do; instead it names specific peoples: Seir (Edom or Idumea), the Philistines (the sea peoples of old, or perhaps the Greeks in Ben Sira's day), and "the foolish people that live in Shechem" (Samaritans). Shechem, of course, was the traditional cultic center for the Samaritans. What may have linked these three peoples together is the perception that they were enemies of Judeans or had somehow harmed the people of Judea like Ben Sira. That impression is strengthened by the allusion to the disdain that Judeans showed to Samaritans when Ben Sira calls them "not even a people." What makes this final numerical saying even more peculiar is that it does not serve as an occasion for further development by Ben Sira or as a part of a longer wisdom instruction. Was it added to Ben Sira's text at some point? If so, by whom, when, and why?

Questions and Answers

Ben Sira begins a short reflection on persons who deserve honor (10:19-25) with a set of four questions and the proper responses to them. The first question appears twice in 10:19: "Whose offspring are worthy of honor?" The first answer is "human offspring," while the second response is "those who fear the Lord." The second question also appears twice: "Whose offspring are unworthy of honor?" The first answer is "human offspring," while the second response is "those who break the commandments."

Ben Sira uses this question-and-answer drill device to introduce a large unit on honor and shame (10:19–11:6). The content of the exercise highlights his recurrent themes of fear of the Lord and keeping God's commandments. What follows in 10:20-25 is a series of teachings stating in different ways that the real source of honor and glory for all persons is fear of the Lord: "The rich and the eminent, and the poor—their glory is the fear of the Lord" (10:22).

The use of the alternating questions and answers is reminiscent of a drill in which the teacher asks questions and the students respond in unison. Such an exercise livens up a class, brings a group together, emphasizes the importance of the material, and drills it into the minds of students. Do we have an echo of one of Ben Sira's "classroom" teaching methods here?

Refrains

Related to the question-and-answer drill format is Ben Sira's use of repetitive phrases or refrains. For example, in 2:7-9 he addresses prospective seekers after wisdom three times in a row with the phrase "You who fear the Lord." Likewise in 2:15-17 he describes the attitudes and actions of genuine seekers after wisdom in three consecutive verses that begin with "Those who fear the Lord." And in a section (19:13-19) pertaining to cases in which a friend or neighbor has been accused of some kind of misconduct Ben Sira prefaces four contiguous sayings with the alternating refrains "Question a friend" (19:13, 15) and "Question a neighbor" (19:14, 17). All these devices help to get the attention of students and readers, and facilitate the memorization and retention of the content. Again we seem to have remnants of Ben Sira's "classroom" practice.

"There Is" Sayings

Another of Ben Sira's characteristic modes of teaching is through "there is" sayings in which the sentence begins in Hebrew with the so-called existential particle *yesh,* and in Greek with *estin,* the third-person singular form of the verb "to be." Since this construction gets obscured in the *NRSV* and other translations I will present more literal renderings when discussing these sayings. In every case the "there is" sayings in Sirach (11:11-13; 20:5-6, and 20:10) draw a contrast.

In 11:11-13 the two "there is" sayings underscore the good advice given in the beginning of the unit against busying oneself excessively with too many matters. On the one hand "there is one who works and struggles and hurries, but is so much the more in want" (11:11). On the other hand "there is one who is slow and needs help, who lacks strength and abounds in poverty" (11:12a). Nevertheless, God may look kindly on the latter and lift him out of lowliness and raise him up "to the amazement of many" (11:12b-13).

A double "there is" construction appears in 20:5-6 in a collection of sayings about speech and silence. According to 20:5 "there is one who keeps silent and is thought to be wise, and there is one who is detested for being talkative" And according to 20:6 "there is one who keeps silent because he has nothing to say, and there is one who keeps silent because he knows when to speak." The sayings capture some of the ambiguity of silence in the sense that people may be silent for very different reasons. Another double "there is" construction occurs in 20:10: "There is a gift that profits you nothing, and there is a gift to be paid back double." The saying reminds us of the experience of receiving "white elephant" gifts that are useless or even worse.

"Better Than" Sayings

While "better than" proverbs are found elsewhere in ancient Near Eastern wisdom writings, in 40:18-27 Ben Sira uses the basic form in a distinctive way. The passage is a series of ten comparisons, culminating in the praise of "fear of the Lord" as the best thing of all. Each of the comparisons consists of two units (see 40:18) in which the first unit contains two nouns ("wealth and wages make life sweet"), while the second unit consists of the expression "but better than either" and an indication of what is even more valuable ("finding a treasure"). The content of the comparisons helps us to understand what Ben Sira considered to be most important in life. The series starts out on a pragmatic, common-sense, and even mundane note. It is true that most people would rather find a treasure than have to work hard and earn money so as to enjoy the "sweet life" (40:18). But soon there appear on Ben Sira's list the familiar topics of wisdom (40:19a), the good wife (40:19b, 23), love of friends (40:20), almsgiving (40:24), and good counsel (40:25). Since green shoots of grain (40:22) promise an abundant harvest they are judged "better than" the momentary pleasure that the eye may derive from looking at "grace and beauty."

Everything mentioned in the first units of the ten comparisons is "good": wealth and wages, children and the building of a city, cattle and orchards, wine and music, and so on. But what appears in the second unit is "better than" them. What is by far the best of all, according to Ben Sira, is "fear of the Lord." This theme occurs in the climactic final position: "riches and strength build up confidence, but fear of the Lord is better than either" (40:26a). To reinforce the point Ben Sira adds two more sayings to the effect that fear of the Lord knows "no want" (40:26b) and covers a person "better than any glory" (40:26c).

Attached to the series of ten "better than" sayings is a short instruction about the evils of being a beggar: "it is better to die than to beg" (40:28). Ben Sira develops that saying in 40:29-30 by noting that being dependent on the kindness of others damages one's self-respect and leads to smoldering resentment (unless one is totally shameless).

Prohibitions

One of the most common forms of speech in Sirach is the prohibition, that is, a sentence with a negative particle and cast in the second person ("Do not . . .") that discourages or forbids certain attitudes or kinds of conduct. Since prohibitions are so common in Sirach, a few examples will suffice to illustrate their basic literary features and their function. The literary scene implied by the prohibitions is that of the senior sage drawing on his long experience and observation of life and imparting to junior or prospective sages what he has learned. The form of these sayings conjures up the image of an elderly man with long gray beard drawing himself up, pointing his finger, and delivering a solemn warning to a young person.

While some prohibitions stand alone in the midst of a large unit, Ben Sira often presents his prohibitions in clusters. For example, in 1:28-30 there are three prohibitions beginning with "Do not" against disregarding the fear of the Lord and approaching God with a divided mind (1:28), being a hypocrite (1:29), and exalting oneself (1:30). And in 4:1-6 Ben Sira adopts the "instruction" mode ("my child"), presents five prohibitions beginning with "Do not" that warn against mistreating the poor and needy (4:1-5), and concludes in 4:6 with a (somewhat strange) motive or reason for observing the prohibitions: "for if in bitterness of soul some should curse you, their Creator will hear their prayer" (4:6). However, in many cases (see 4:30) no motive or reason for the prohibition is given: "Do not be like a lion in your home, or suspicious of your servants." The idea is that the listener will be able to grasp the point and apply some reason for it.

The prohibitions in Sirach and other wisdom books are put forward as wise guides to thinking and living. Based on experience and observation, they aim to keep those being instructed on the straight and narrow path toward wisdom. While most of the prohibitions are negative in the sense of warning against certain attitudes or behaviors, sometimes the effect is to encourage positive action. For example, in 4:23 Ben Sira uses the "Do not" formula to encourage the younger sage to speak up at the right time: "Do not refrain from speaking at the proper moment, and do not hide your wisdom." This "prohibition" is accompanied in 4:24 with a rationale for why one should speak up: "for wisdom becomes known through speech, and education through the words of the tongue." Indeed, one of the goals of the scribal education offered by Ben Sira is to prepare younger or prospective sages to discern the proper moment in which to speak and to provide them with an arsenal of tried and tested wise sayings that they might use in such a situation.

One concrete and lively use of the "prohibition" form occurs in 5:1-8. This is Ben Sira's brilliant presentation of the psychology of sinners who commit immoral actions and explain them away in various forms of denial. One of Ben Sira's strengths as a teacher was to look into the mind and heart of sinners, to describe how they try to deceive others, to list the excuses they customarily offer, and to show how their efforts at deception end badly for them and those around them. Each verse in the passage begins with the "Do not" formula. At several points (5:1, 3, 4, 6) Ben Sira warns ("Do not say . . .") against what sinners commonly say in their own defense: "I have enough [wealth]," as if one could buy oneself out of trouble; "Who can have power over me?" as if one could escape the power of God; "I have sinned, yet what has happened to me?" as if the absence of immediate consequences somehow justifies the sin; and "His [God's] mercy is great, he will forgive the multitude of my sins," as if one could presume upon

God's mercy. Thus Ben Sira creates a dialogue (or diatribe) between sinners defending their actions and the biblical tradition. At each point he reveals the inadequacy and foolishness of sinners who try to justify their presumptuous attitudes and behaviors with regard to sin and to God's justice and mercy.

Instructions

The instruction was a common literary form for conveying wisdom teachings in the ancient Near East. The "Words of the Wise" in Prov 22:17–24:22 (which seems to depend on an even earlier Egyptian proto-type) and the work found at Qumran and now known as 4QInstruction are sustained examples of the genre. The instruction form is quite flexible in that in the *persona* of the authoritative sage a wisdom teacher is able to combine maxims or proverbs, admonitions, prohibitions, motive clauses, and many other forms of teaching (even some based on biblical texts).

Ben Sira frequently used the instruction form as a vehicle for present-ing various teachings—some clearly traditional, and other perhaps original—on a single topic. Thus his instructions function as something like para-graphs on a single topic. They usually begin with a direct address such as "my son/child" or "O children" (see 2:1; 3:1; 3:17; 4:1; etc.). The address reflects Ben Sira's status as an experienced teacher who instructs young men who want to become sages like him. In the Hebrew and Greek ver-sions the language is masculine, since it appears that all the students in Ben Sira's school were young males. Modern translations like the *NRSV* now use more gender-inclusive language such as "my child" to indicate their potential significance for both men and women today.

The instruction form serves as a device for gathering small packets of wisdom under one heading, and allows for a more concentrated reflection on a particular topic. The instruction about "fear of the Lord" in 2:1-18 be-gins with "my son" and treats different aspects of the theme in six short units. The instruction about parents and children in 3:1-16 takes as its start-ing point the biblical commandments about honoring one's parents (Exod 20:12; Deut 5:16), and offers many reasons why doing so is a wise thing. Likewise, the instruction about humility in 3:17-29 develops the topic in terms of admonitions about humility in one's actions (3:17-20) and warn-ings against intellectual pride (3:21-24; 3:25-29).

Prayers of Petition

It is unusual to find prayers of petition in a wisdom book. The two such prayers in Sirach—one an individual petition and the other a communal petition—are directed to the God of Israel who is also the "Lord of all."

The prayer of petition in 22:27–23:6 serves to introduce more conventional wisdom instructions about disciplining the tongue (23:7-15) and about sexual sins (23:16-27). By prefacing these two instructions with a prayer of petition Ben Sira highlights the gravity of these sins and suggests that without God's aid no one can overcome them. This individually oriented prayer asks for divine help in avoiding sins connected with speech and sexual sins. It is structured according to a twofold question (22:27; 23:2-3) and petition (23:1; 23:4-6) pattern. The one who makes this prayer first asks who will set a guard over his mouth, lips, and tongue lest he fall into sins of speech and be destroyed (22:27). Then he addresses God as "Father and master of my life," and prays that God not abandon him and let him fall because of them (23:1). Next the petitioner asks who will discipline his thoughts and mind concerning sexual matters ("hot passion") lest he be ashamed before his enemies (23:2-3). Then he calls upon God as the "Lord, Father and God of my life," and prays that God might remove "evil desire" and not give him over to "shameless passion" (23:4-6).

The second prayer of petition (36:1-22) follows a description of God as a powerful warrior meting out justice to the wicked and merciless (35:22b-26). This communually oriented prayer asks God to show mercy to his people (36:1-12) and to gather them into Jerusalem and its Temple (36:13-22). The prayer addresses the "God of all" (36:1) and affirms that there is "no God but you, O Lord" (36:5). Using biblical phrases, the prayer asks God to have mercy on Israel and to "put the nations in fear of you" (36:2). It recalls the events surrounding ancient Israel's exodus from Egypt and asks for "new signs and . . . other wonders." It begs God to show forth his glory now, and so put to shame those who say, "there is no one but ourselves" (36:12). The second part of the prayer (36:13-22) asks for God to gather in all Israel and to bless the Temple in Jerusalem. When God's promises and prophecies are fulfilled in Israel, all the nations will know that "you are the Lord, the God of the ages" (36:22). Both parts of the prayer suggest that it is in God's own interest that he crush Israel's enemies and restore his people to greatness, since his honor and glory are at stake.

Hymns

It is also unusual to find hymns in ancient Near Eastern wisdom books. While it is unlikely that the "hymns" in Sirach were ever meant to be sung in a community setting, they do use the literary conventions of hymns. The best example comes in 42:15–43:33, just before the "Praise of the Fathers" in chapters 44–49. If a hymn is a song of praise or adoration, this passage fits the definition. Using first-person singular language, Ben Sira proposes to "call to mind the works of the Lord, and . . . declare what I have seen." He affirms that "by the word of the Lord his works are made," thus echoing Genesis 1 and Sirach 24, while looking forward to 43:26b: "by his word all things hold together." The first part of the hymn (42:15–25) praises God's creation as "full of his glory" and celebrates God's omniscient and purposeful governance of creation. The second part (43:1-12) reflects on God's glory made manifest in the heavenly bodies: the sun, the moon, the stars, and the rainbow. The third part (43:13-26) celebrates God's glory revealed in the elements of nature: snow, lightning, clouds, hailstones, thunder, and so on. The fourth section (43:27-33) proposes as the "final word" about God the affirmation "He is the all," and invites everyone to join in the hymn of praise: "glorify the Lord and exalt him as much as you can, for he surpasses even that" (43:30).

Another hymnic passage (51:1-12) takes the form of a classic thanksgiving hymn. The Greek textual tradition includes the heading "Prayer of Jesus Son of Sirach." But nothing in the hymn itself demands that it was written by Ben Sira, and in tone and content it is quite different from anything that Ben Sira says about himself in the body of the book. This thanksgiving hymn begins with the customary formulas: "I give you thanks, O Lord and King, and praise you, O God my savior. I give thanks to your name" (51:1). Then, again following the biblical model, the speaker describes the dangers of slander and the false accusation he has endured (51:2-6a), and narrates how he came to turn to God in prayer (51:6b-10). Finally he praises God for having rescued him and promises to give thanks to God continually (51:11-12), though without explicit mention of material sacrifices.

Other texts in Sirach incorporate hymnic elements but are mixed in their literary forms. In 39:12-35 Ben Sira issues a solemn call to "ascribe majesty to his name and give thanks to him with praise" (39:15). He ends with still another call to "sing praise with all your heart and voice, and bless the name of the Lord" (39:35). But the bulk of the passage is Ben Sira's discourse on creation and on how the necessities of life are good for the godly but evil for sinners. Here the hymnic elements are used rhetorically to lend emphasis to what Ben Sira regarded as an important and original piece of his theological thinking.[3]

Likewise, near the end of the main text there is in 50:22-24 the call to "bless the God of all" because of his power in creation, providential care,

[3] See Jan Liesen, *Full of Praise: An Exegetical Study of Sir 39,12-35*. JSJSup 64 (Leiden: Brill, 1999).

and mercy. But this benediction/hymn quickly turns into a series of petitions that ask God to give his people joy, peace, mercy, and deliverance. Again the hymnic elements serve rhetorically to round off the description of Simon the high priest (50:1-21) and mark the transition to the close of the book.

Ben Sira's inclusion of prayers and hymns in his wisdom book reinforces his conviction that human wisdom should be taught and learned in the framework of divine wisdom and fear of the Lord. When reflecting on his own quest for wisdom when he was young, he recalls: "I sought wisdom openly in my prayer" (51:13). And he expected that his own ideal student would pray regularly: "He sets his heart to rise early to seek the Lord who made him, and to petition the Most High; he opens his mouth in prayer and asks pardon for his sins" (39:5). For Ben Sira worldly wisdom and spirituality come from God and are best nurtured in an atmosphere of prayer.

Praise of Wisdom (Aretalogy)

In 24:1-22 Wisdom appears as a female figure present both in the heavenly assembly and on earth. The heading "the Praise of Wisdom" appears in Greek manuscripts of the book. But the passage is not so much a poem about Wisdom as it is Wisdom's praise of herself in the first person singular ("I"). The literary form of self-praise in which one recites one's own excellence and virtues is sometimes called an "aretalogy." The aretalogy is especially connected in Greco-Roman times with the cult of the Egyptian goddess Isis that spread rapidly across the Mediterraean world.

In 24:3-7 Wisdom narrates her origin ("I came forth from the mouth of the Most High") and her search for a dwelling place. Next, in 24:8-12, she tells how God assigned for her a dwelling place in the Jerusalem Temple. Then in a series of similes Wisdom in 24:13-17 compares her beauty to tall trees (24:13-14), sweet smelling spices (24:15), branches on a tree (24:16), and a budding vine (24:17). Finally, in 24:19-22 Wisdom issues an invitation to come and enjoy her banquet. It is possible that Ben Sira was deliberately using the literary form of aretalogy to assert Wisdom's superiority over Isis or some other goddess.

While the personification of Wisdom goes back to Prov 8:22-31, Sir 24:1-22 is far more definitive regarding Wisdom's dwelling place on earth. She dwells in the Jerusalem Temple. Ben Sira, of course, lived in Jerusalem (50:27), and provides a glowing description of a Temple liturgy there in 50:5-24. It is possible that his own school was associated with the Temple complex as a kind of "seminary." In his comment following the aretalogy Ben Sira makes a momentous claim: "All this [Wisdom] is the book of the covenant of the Most High God, the law that Moses commanded us as an inheritance for the congregation of Jacob" (24:23). In other words, Wisdom is the Torah. That claim is central to Ben Sira's effort at joining the distinctively Jewish Torah tradition and the more secular wisdom tradition of the ancient Near East.

Rewritten Bible

Chapters 44–49 form a coherent and distinctive unit in the book of Sirach.[4] Often referred to from its first words, "Now let us praise famous men," the passage sings the praises of various biblical heroes from Enoch to Nehemiah. It is preceded by a "hymn" in praise of God's works in nature (42:15–43:33), and leads into Ben Sira's description of Simon the High Priest presiding at a worship service in the Jerusalem Temple (50:5-24). The main source for this parade of heroes was, of course, the Hebrew Bible. In almost all cases Ben Sira picks out a few items from the biblical narrative and weaves them into his rewriting of biblical history in order to show how these figures reflected the glory of God.

The practice of paraphrasing or summarizing biblical texts was becoming popular in Ben Sira's time. The most extensive effort at rewriting the Bible was Josephus' *Jewish Antiquities,* whose twenty books constitute a history of Israel from Adam to the first century C.E. But there are other examples such as the Qumran *Genesis Apocryphon, Jubilees,* Pseudo-Philo's *Biblical Antiquities,* and the Aramaic Targums of the Hebrew Bible. Sometimes those who rewrote the Bible did so simply to solve exegetical problems in the text, but very often there was a theological or polemical point to be made.

Ben Sira's brief treatment of Abraham in 44:19-21 illustrates the literary form and some features of his theological approach to the Bible. He begins in 44:19 by calling Abraham "the great father of a multitude of nations" (Gen 17:4-5) and declaring him to be incomparable in glory. But instead of making Abraham into a "universal" figure as Paul does in Romans 4, Ben Sira in 44:20 emphasizes his distinctive Jewish identity. He insists that Abraham observed the law of the Most High (see Gen 26:5—even before the law was given to Moses on Sinai), that God took Abraham into "the covenant in his flesh" (circumcision; see Gen 17:1-21), and that Abraham passed the "test" God put before him when he ordered Abraham to

---

[4] See Burton L. Mack, *Wisdom and the Hebrew Epic: Ben Sira's Hymn in Praise of the Fathers* (Chicago: University of Chicago Press, 1985); and Thomas R. Lee, *Studies in the Form of Sirach 44–50.* SBLDS 75 (Atlanta: Scholars, 1986).

sacrifice his son Isaac (Gen 22:1-19). According to Ben Sira, Abraham became the father of many nations because he kept the law, entered into the covenant of circumcision, and was found faithful in his testing (44:21). In this treatment of Abraham it is possible that Ben Sira was reacting against attempts by Hellenizing Jews (see 1 Macc 1:11-15) to put aside the distinctive features of Judaism (such as Torah observance and male circumcision) by appealing to Abraham as a "universal" figure apart from his Judaism. Ben Sira, however, goes in the opposite direction, and underlines the Jewishness of Abraham in his "rewriting" of the biblical accounts pertaining to Abraham.

Conclusion

Ben Sira the teacher presents his wisdom with an array of literary forms. Our analysis has proceeded from smaller forms (maxims or proverbs, beatitudes, woes, etc.) to larger forms (prayers of petition, hymns, rewritten Bible). In the question-and-answer and refrain forms we can discern possible echoes of Ben Sira's classroom practices. Many of these forms lend themselves to easy memorization, thus supplying Ben Sira's students with a storehouse of wisdom by which to conduct themselves wisely and to interpret the world around them. The various literary forms contribute nicely to Ben Sira's program of integrating secular wisdom and biblical wisdom. Stripped of their particularity and context in life, they can sound abstract and sterile. But since they invite reflection and actualization on the reader's part, these literary forms were highly appropriate for the kind of moral formation Ben Sira had in mind. They are further indications that Ben Sira was an imaginative and effective pedagogue.

CHAPTER FIVE

Ben Sira's Social World

Ben Sira was a man of his time and place. And as all peoples do, the people of his time and place made certain assumptions about who was worthy of honor, about family life and the structure of the household, about the status of various persons and professions in society, and about public behavior and financial transactions. In some matters Ben Sira seems to have accepted their assumptions without much questioning, while in other cases he challenged them or least relativized them in the name of the transcendent values of divine wisdom and fear of the Lord.

The book of Sirach offers a window onto how an upper-class Judean wisdom teacher in the early second century B.C.E. viewed the social order of the world in which he lived and worked. Ben Sira had opinions about practically all realms of life and expressed them freely. He resided in the land of Israel, which at least since Alexander the Great's conquest in the mid-fourth century B.C.E. had been part of the broader Mediterranean culture. However much Ben Sira may have opposed the inroads of "Hellenism," he was part of it and was influenced by it.[1] Moreover, though a city dweller, Ben Sira functioned in a predominantly agrarian society, which did not change much over the centuries. And his social world was not much different from the social world of Jesus of Nazareth and his first followers some two hundred years later.

Ben Sira's book is a rich resource (a social historian's "gold mine") for those who wish to explore the social assumptions and structures of ancient Mediterranean society (social description). He provides abundant documentation for the major features in that worldview. This chapter

---

[1] See Martin Hengel, *Judaism and Hellenism* (Philadelphia: Fortress, 1975) 1:131–53; and Jack T. Sanders, *Ben Sira and Demotic Wisdom.* SBLMS 28 (Chico: Scholars, 1983).

focuses on four such features: honor and shame, the patriarchal household, the social hierarchy, and social relations. In Ben Sira's world it was very important to have one's significance validated by others (honor) and to avoid "losing face" before others (shame). In the household the father was expected to rule supreme and to exercise authority over his wife, children, and slaves (patriarchy). His society was hierarchical, with each person occupying a position largely based on family pedigree, property, and wealth. There was not much room for upward social mobility (social hierarchy). And in social situations—speaking in public, eating with others, financial transactions, and living alongside others in harmony, it was important not to look bad or to diminish one's reputation. To use a modern analogy, Ben Sira's social world was more like that of "Tony Soprano" and the "Godfather" than the one that most of us inhabit.

The social world of Ben Sira was very different from that of most readers of this book. Whereas we prize our individuality and autonomy, people in Ben Sira's social world perceived themselves as embedded in a group (family, clan, village or city, etc.) and judged their own importance (honored or shamed) by what other people thought of them. Whereas we may assume that all people are equal, Ben Sira's social world was hierarchical, with everyone having a relatively fixed place in the social order. Whereas we may regard men and women as equals, Ben Sira's social world considered wives to be naturally subordinate to their husbands, and children (and slaves) as naturally subordinate to the head of the household *(paterfamilias)*.

Ben Sira's opinions on many social matters, especially his comments on women (see 25:16; 42:14), will strike most modern readers as benighted or even outrageous. At least something in this chapter will get every modern reader angry. Many of these opinions may be due to the social assumptions he shared with his contemporaries. And that is our main concern here. But some of his more egregious statements may also reflect his intention to speak directly to the original audience for his teachings—young Jewish males on the way to becoming scribes/sages. Still others (as with his views on women) may reflect his own unhappy experiences or even his personal pathology (misogyny).

In defense of Ben Sira, it is important to notice that on several topics treated under the rubric of "social description" he turns out to be "countercultural" to some extent, insofar as he repeatedly places the search for wisdom and fear of the Lord above material possessions, authority over others, and honor from others. Even in these most controversial matters Ben Sira can still be a wise guide in at least two ways: He helps us to see what people in his time and place took for granted about their society and about social relations, and he shows us how a serious Jewish religious teacher counseled his students to pursue wisdom and fear of the Lord above all else.

Honor and Shame

Social scientists define honor as a claim to worth that is publicly acknowledged. Shame is the opposite of honor.[2] Shame means having one's claim to honor rejected and ridiculed in the public forum. Ben Sira lived in a society in which one's worth or importance depended largely on what other persons thought and on one's place within the larger society. To *be* honored was to have one's worth acclaimed by others. To *have* honor was to have one's value or skill recognized by others. To *be* shamed was to have one's claim to worth exposed as fraudulent or to have one's sense of worth stripped away. However, to *have* shame can prevent one from attitudes and behaviors that might bring shame. Honor and shame depend to a large extent on the social context. If no one regards certain attitudes or behaviors as worthy of honor, those who act in those ways will not be honored and so will not have honor. Likewise, if nothing is considered as shameful, then there will be no shame.

Ben Sira lived in an honor-shame society, one in which certain attitudes and behaviors were recognized as honorable and others were viewed as shameful. As a wisdom teacher, Ben Sira was preparing young men to be public figures well trained in both the biblical and the sapiential traditions. He regarded the profession of the "scribe" (something like our "public intellectual" today) as the noblest and most honorable role in his second century B.C.E. Jewish society.

Since honor and shame depend to a large extent on their social context (what others think), Ben Sira took as his task to delineate what attitudes and behaviors constitute the truly honorable and shameful. His explicit teachings on honor and shame appear for the most part in three long passages: 4:20–6:4; 10:19–11:6; and 41:14–42:8. His goal in these instructions is to rescue honor and shame from the changing *mores* of society and the whims of the general public, and to give these social values a firm foundation in the unchanging religious values of wisdom, the commandments, and the fear of the Lord.

---

[2] See David deSilva, "The Wisdom of Ben Sira: Honor, Shame, and the Maintenance of the Values of a Minority Culture," *CBQ* 58 (1996) 433–55. For general information about this approach to ancient texts see Bruce J. Malina, *The New Testament World: Insights from Cultural Anthropology* (3rd, rev. ed. Louisville: Westminster John Knox, 2001); and John J. Pilch and Bruce J. Malina, eds., *Handbook of Biblical Social Values* (Peabody, MA: Hendrickson, 1998).

In 4:20-21 Ben Sira begins his exhortation (4:20–6:4) by urging his readers: "do not be ashamed to be yourself," thus relativizing the opinions of others and embracing the values of self-acceptance and personal integrity. He goes on to distinguish between "a shame that leads to sin"— sins that result from covert actions—and "a shame that is glory and favor," in which fear of public exposure may prevent one from committing sins. Ben Sira recognized that in an honor-shame society individuals do not always have to follow the rules. Indeed, one of his favorite themes is free will. He insists that a person can and must choose to act wisely and justly or to act foolishly and sin. In his teachings Ben Sira frequently appeals to considerations of honor and shame as motivations for good and wise conduct. However, he also stresses the superiority of acting out of fear of the Lord (the religious dimension) and of doing the right thing (the moral dimension). Thus he tries to move his students and readers beyond the realm of social convention and public opinion to the more explicitly theological and moral levels of behavior.

Much of the exhortation that follows in 4:22–6:4 concerns the attitudes and behaviors Ben Sira regards as truly honorable and truly shameful. Making frequent use of the prohibition form ("do not"), Ben Sira in 4:22-31 refers to the kinds of speech that may bring honor or shame, and emerges as a champion of speaking the truth: "Fight to the death for truth, and the Lord God will fight for you" (4:28). At the center of his exhortation (5:1-8) he gives a remarkably insightful presentation of the psychology of the sinner in which he rebuts the various excuses and denials customarily used to explain away sinful actions. Then in 5:9–6:1 he returns to the theme of speech: "Honor and dishonor come from speaking, and the tongue of mortals may be their downfall" (5:13). He reserves his harshest criticism for the "double-tongued" (5:14; 6:1), most likely a reference to the slanderer. He concludes by pointing to "passion" as the root of shameful attitudes and behaviors, and shows how passion can and does destroy persons: "Evil passion destroys those who have it, and makes them the laughingstock of their enemies" (6:4).

The second exhortation (10:19–11:6) on honor and shame continues Ben Sira's program of redefining honor and shame not in terms of wealth, power, and social status but rather in terms of wisdom, keeping the commandments, and the fear of the Lord. Using the question-and-answer drill format, Ben Sira in 10:19 identifies those who fear the Lord as "worthy of honor" and those who break the commandments as "unworthy of honor." Without denying that princes, judges, and rulers deserve honor, he affirms that "none of them is greater than the one who fears the Lord" (10:24). Neither good looks (11:2) nor fine clothes (11:4) brings true honor. On the contrary, the honor that is available to everyone resides in the pursuit of knowledge and wisdom. At the same time Ben Sira urges modesty and caution even among those who find honor in this way: "My child, honor yourself with humility . . . and do not exalt yourself when you are honored" (10:28; 11:4). He bids them to reflect on the many examples of kings and rulers who have found themselves defeated and disgraced (11:5-6).

What brings honor and shame to a person depends on what people in a particular society regard as honorable and shameful. Again in 41:14–42:8 Ben Sira seeks to redefine the values of his society and to place them on solid religious and moral foundations. In 41:17–42:1a he gives a list of actions that should bring shame and of the persons before whom one should be ashamed to do them (parents, colleagues, etc.). The list of shameful actions includes sexual immorality, lying, criminal behavior, unjust dealing, theft, breaking oaths or agreements, impolite behavior ("leaning on your elbow at meals"), surliness in receiving or giving, rudeness ("silence before those who greet you"), looking at a prostitute, rejecting the appeal of a relative, taking away someone's portion or gift, gazing at another man's wife or "meddling" with his servant girl, abusive words, insulting after making a gift, repeating gossip, and betraying secrets. In Ben Sira's view these are the things that should bring shame. And if these behaviors are avoided, "then you will show proper shame and will find favor with everyone" (42:1a).

The list of shameful things is complemented by another list of things not to be ashamed of in 42:1b-8. What heads this list is "the law of the Most High and his covenant." In this list Ben Sira urges ethical business practices, careful supervision over members of one's family and household, and willingness to correct sinners. These are the behaviors that should win true honor: "Then you will show your sound training and will be approved by all" (42:8b).

The Patriarchal Household

Ben Sira lived in a male-centered or patriarchal society. In his school for prospective sages the students seem to have been males intent on making their way in the world. The implicit reader of the book is a bright young Jewish man with every expectation of becoming the "head" or patriarch of his own household. What Ben Sira says about the members of a family or household is always and entirely from the perspective of the male head of a household. It is assumed that this *paterfamilias* will oversee all the other members, keeping everyone and everything under his control and fulfilling his obligations toward them. By doing so the patriarch will avoid shame and increase his own honor in his world.

Several passages scattered throughout the book of Sirach form a kind of "household code"—a literary form found in Aristotle's *Nicomachean Ethics* and picked up and "christianized" in Col 3:18–4:1 and Eph 5:21–6:9. These passages describe the relations and obligations of the patriarch to the various members of his household.

Topic 1: Parents (3:1-16). After reflecting on the nature of wisdom and on the fear of the Lord in Sirach 1–2, Ben Sira treats duties toward parents in 3:1-16. His starting point is the biblical commandment to "honor your father and your mother" (Exod 20:12; Deut 5:16). He is especially concerned to give further reasons why one should obey that commandment. Ben Sira recognized that the biblical commandment was addressed primarily to adult children with regard to their aging or aged parents. In addition to the biblical promise of a long life, he contends that such conduct fits with the divine plan or economy ("the Lord honors a father above his children," 3:2), atones for sins (3:3), shapes one's own family in positive ways (3:5a), prompts God to answer one's prayers (3:5b), and constitutes obedience to God (3:6).

In 3:8-11 Ben Sira places this commandment in the context of honor and shame. Those who honor their parents will receive a blessing from them (and not a curse), whereas dishonoring one's parents brings dishonor and disgrace upon the offending adult child. In 3:12-16 Ben Sira brings up the case of an elderly parent who needs special care, particularly "if his mind fails" (3:13). Ben Sira promises that those who care for such parents will be rewarded by God: "For kindness to a father will not be forgotten, and will be credited to you against your sins" (3:14). On the contrary, according to 3:16 whoever abandons a father is like a "blasphemer," and whoever angers a mother is "cursed by God." In a society in which life expectancies were relatively short, Ben Sira's advice on this matter is sensitive and humane, and seems especially relevant for people today where the care of aging parents is a reality for more people than ever before.

Topic 2: Women and Marriage (36:26-31; 25:13–26:27). The young men addressed by Ben Sira were expected and encouraged to marry, if for no other reason than the practical one of giving stability to their lives: "where there is no wife, a man will become a fugitive and a wanderer" (36:30). At their social level it is likely that their marriages were arranged between the patriarchs of their households. However, the young man apparently had some say in the process, at least more than the young woman did. Ben Sira is annoyingly cavalier about this: "A woman will accept any man as a husband, but one girl is preferable to another" (36:26).[3]

[3] See Warren C. Trenchard, *Ben Sira's View of Women: A Literary Analysis.* BJS 38 (Chico: Scholars, 1982).

The best combination in a prospective wife is her physical beauty ("a woman's beauty lights up a man's face, and there is nothing he desires more," 36:27) and a good (submissive) disposition ("kindness and humility mark her speech," 36:28). According to Ben Sira a good wife is a man's "best possession, a helper fit for him and a pillar of support" (36:29).

The relative merits of a "good wife" and a "bad wife" are the subjects of the long instruction in 25:13–26:27. The passage presents alternating descriptions of a wicked woman/wife (25:13-26; 26:5-12) and a good wife (26:1-4; 26:13-18), along with a concluding combined reflection on the bad wife and the good wife in 26:19-27. While Ben Sira is certainly a "male chauvinist," he also shows sensitivity to what a positive force a good wife can be in a man's life.

Ben Sira's first description of the wicked woman/bad wife (25:13-26) is summarized in one of his most notorious sayings: "I would rather live with a lion and a dragon than live with an evil woman" (25:16). He warns his male readers to beware of garrulous women ("a sandy ascent for the feet of the aged," 25:20), and not to be ensnared by a woman's beauty or possessions. One of his major concerns is that such a wife will make a man unhappy, and so he will be shamed before his male colleagues. In Ben Sira's view it is especially shameful ("wrath and impudence and great disgrace," 25:22) that a husband should be supported by his wife. In a rare move in the biblical tradition Ben Sira blames Eve alone for the "original sin" and its consequences: "From a woman sin had its beginning, and because of her we all die" (25:24; see Gen 3:6; 1 Tim 2:14). The only escape for a husband in his misery because of his wife is divorce, which was a strategy available only to the husband under the Mosaic Law: "If she does not go as you direct, separate her from yourself" (25:26).

The second description of the wicked woman/bad wife (26:5-12) compares living with such a one to a "chafing yoke" and to grasping a scorpion (26:7), and singles out her drunkenness and unchastity as especially painful and shameful to her husband. By contrast, Ben Sira gives the highest praise to the "good wife," though of course from the male's perspective. The husband of a good wife, according to 26:1-4, will live twice as long, and will find joy and peace. Whether rich or poor, the husband of such a wife will experience contentment and joy. In short, for him "a good wife is a great blessing" (26:3). In the same vein, in 26:13-15 Ben Sira lists some characteristics that make the good wife such a blessing: her charm and skill (in cooking), silence and self-discipline, and modesty and chastity. Then in 26:16-18 he compares her physical beauty to the sun rising upon the mountains, her face to a lamp shining on a holy lampstand, and her legs and feet to golden pillars on silver bases.

In light of these contrasting portraits Ben Sira urges his readers to choose one woman, to marry her, and to have children by her (26:19-21). At the same time, he urges caution regarding relationships with prostitutes and married women, as well as all godless, shameless, and headstrong women. Again, the male's honor and shame are major concerns: "A wife honoring her husband will seem wise to all, but if she dishonors him in her pride she will be known to all as ungodly" (26:26).

Topic 3: Sons and Daughters (30:1-13; 26:10-12; 42:9-14). With regard to raising sons, Ben Sira urges strict discipline. Again what is at stake is the father's honor: "Discipline your son and make his yoke heavy, so that you may not be offended by his shamelessness" (30:13). In 30:1-6 Ben Sira recounts the positive effects of applying strict discipline to his son: "He who loves his son will whip him often, so that he may rejoice at the way he turns out" (30:1). During his father's lifetime the well-disciplined son will be a source of honor. And after his father's death the well-disciplined son will be able to take his father's place, even to the point of avenging his father's enemies and repaying his friends.

On the contrary, according to 30:7-12 one who spoils a son will suffer greatly for it: "Pamper a child, and he will terrorize you" (30:9). The ideal father is a distant and forbidding figure, ready to correct and punish whenever necessary. The concept of a father being his son's friend is repugnant to Ben Sira: "play with him, and he will grieve you" (30:9). For him a son is like an animal (a dog in our culture) who needs to be trained and domesticated.

According to Ben Sira daughters present even greater headaches than sons do. The patriarch's greatest fear in 26:10-12 is that the daughter will engage in promiscuous sexual relations: "she will sit in front of every tent peg and open her quiver to the arrow" (26:12). One problem for the father is that such a daughter will make herself unacceptable for any arranged marriage (because she is not a virgin).

In 42:9-14 Ben Sira reflects on what a constant source of anxiety a daughter presents to her father (42:9-10): When she is young he fears she will not be married; when she is married he fears that her husband will send her back to his household; when she is a virgin he fears she will get pregnant; and when she is married he fears she will commit adultery or not bear children. In light of these fears Ben Sira urges constant vigilance: "Keep strict watch over a headstrong daughter" (42:11). Again what is prominent in his advice is the shame that the father himself might incur: "she may make you a laughingstock to your enemies . . . and put you to shame in public gatherings" (42:12).

Therefore the best strategy for a father is to keep his daughter almost like a prisoner in his own household, away from men and even away from married women on the grounds that "from a woman comes woman's wickedness." (42:13). Ben Sira caps off his instruction about raising daughters with an another notorious saying: "Better is the wickedness of a man than a woman who does good" (42:14a). The outrageous content of this statement can divert attention from the following line that neatly expresses a recurring theme in Ben Sira's household code: "it is woman who brings shame and disgrace" (42:14b). His persistent concern (and even obsession) is with the shame that family members might bring upon the patriarch's honor. Not much attention is given to the well-being, happiness, and growth of other members of the household. While this can be explained in part as due to the primary audience for Ben Sira's teachings (young men), there is little or no recognition of what the patriarch might do positively on behalf of his wife and children.

Topic 4: Managing the Household (33:20-33). The implicit recipient of Ben Sira's instructions about the household is a male with the prospect of becoming the head of a household with property and slaves. In 33:20-24 he warns such a person never to hand on the authority over the household to any other person, be it son, wife, brother, or friend. It is always better that one's children have to ask from their father than vice versa. And so it is better to defer the division of one's property to the hour of one's death. Meanwhile, his advice is to "excel in all that you do; bring no stain upon your honor" (33:23).

The household envisioned in Ben Sira's instruction included slaves, and again his advice about slaves features harsh discipline. In 33:25-30 he urges masters to provide "bread and discipline and work" for their slaves. The secret to treating slaves effectively is to keep them busy, and to punish the recalcitrant ones with "racks and tortures" (33:27). In the case of someone who owns only one slave (33:31-33), however, Ben Sira's advice is more restained and lenient. Since owning only one slave implies a modest household, that slave becomes a precious possession on which the household may depend. If that slave were to run away, the householder might not have the resources to track him down and the household might be in danger of falling apart. Therefore Ben Sira counsels treating him "like yourself" or "like a brother."

The Social Hierarchy

In Ben Sira's social hierarchy the highest position is held by the scribe or sage. Of course, he was one himself, and he conducted a school for training prospective scribes/sages. Trained in both sapiential and biblical traditions, the scribe ideally combined the skills and roles of public intellectual, lawyer, theologian, and politician. While recognizing the indispensable contributions made to society by farmers and artisans, Ben Sira reserves the place at the top of his social hierarchy for the scribe/sage. Even kings and other rulers, if they are to be truly effective and successful, must be wise. His remarkably positive view of the physician offers a neat picture of both physician and patient as dependent on God.

Topic 1: The Sage (38:24–39:11). Ben Sira ran a school for "scribes." He trained young men not only to read and write, but also to master the best of the ancient Near Eastern wisdom tradition and the Scriptures of his people (the Hebrew Bible). He expected that these young men would develop into intellectual and political leaders not only in their local circles but also in what passed for the international (Mediterranean) world of his day. A better word than "scribe" to describe the kind of student Ben Sira sought to produce is the word "sage," a synonym for "wise man." In 38:24–39:11 Ben Sira describes in detail the social value, training, and social functions of the sage.

The sage is a public person capable of exercising leadership in the most important areas of social life. The sage needs the time and leisure in which to search for and find wisdom (38:24). Farmers, craftsmen, smiths, and potters are all necessary for the creation and continuance of the social order (38:25-32). But such persons, no matter how essential their tasks may be, are not sought out for political, legal, and educational leadership (38:33) as the sages are. Their minds and energies are on other (mundane) things.

Besides supplying social leadership, the sage contributes to the preservation of the Jewish religious tradition. The sage devotes himself to the study of the law of the Most High, which involves the wisdom of all the ancients, the prophecies, the discourses of notable persons, the subtleties of parables, the hidden message of proverbs, and the obscurities of parables (39:1-3). Accepting the identification of the Jewish law and wisdom (see 24:23), Ben Sira's sage seeks to understand the law as fully as possible and uses all the intellectual powers at his disposal. Nevertheless, he will be filled with the spirit of understanding and pour forth words of wisdom only if and when "the great Lord is willing" (39:6). Thus the preservation of the religious tradition demands not only the human efforts of the sages but also the inspiring power of God. The spiritual regime of the sage and the results of it are described in 39:6-11. The ultimate reward that the scribe can expect is "a name greater than a thousand" (39:11).

A third function of the sage is glimpsed in 39:4: "he serves among the great and appears before rulers; he travels in foreign lands, and learns what is good and evil in the human lot." Besides being a leader and a scholar, the sage is also a kind of counselor or technical expert for the powerful. He is ready and willing to adjudicate disputes even in foreign lands. For all of Ben Sira's enthusiasm and gratitude for the priests, kings, and prophets of Israel's past (see chs. 44–50), he clearly regards the sage as the most necessary and important person for Jewish society in his own day. Of course, it was to the training of sages that Ben Sira devoted his life.

Topic 2: Wise Rulers (9:17–10:5). A good leader is a wise leader, and wisdom makes a leader good and effective. According to 9:17-18 the most effective instruments a wise leader uses are words, not loud or reckless words but wise words. A wise ruler sees to it that his people are well educated, and the result will be an orderly and wise city: "a city becomes fit to live in through the understanding of its rulers" (10:3). However, as noted in 10:4-5, rule over all the earth is in the hand of God, and Ben Sira is confident that God will raise up the right leaders in crucial times and is the source of all human success. To cap off the instruction, Ben Sira in 10:5 returns to his favorite theme of honor: "it is he [God] who confers honor upon the lawgiver" [or "scribe," according to the Greek version].

Topic 3: Physicians (38:1-15). In the ancient world, and in Ben's Sira's world in particular, what we call "physicians" functioned at a fairly primitive level, had at best moderate success, and were not held in high esteem. Indeed, they are hardly mentioned in the Bible. Ben Sira, however, presents in 38:1-15 a remarkably positive account of physicians, and places their work in a thoroughly religious context. In 38:1-3 Ben Sira urges his readers to "honor physicians for their services, for the Lord created them." He notes that their gift of healing comes "from the Most High," and so they deserve to be held in high esteem and to be honored. In 38:4-8 Ben Sira acknowledges the value of medicines. Since these medicines were all derived from nature (plants, roots, etc.), he can say that God created them and that through the skills of physicians and pharmacists God brings healing all over the world. While emphasizing the cooperation between God and human agents, Ben Sira regards the action of God to be of primary importance.

In the second part (38:9-15) Ben Sira gives advice on what to do when one is ill. In 38:9-11 he first outlines a three-step regimen for "getting right with God": pray to the Lord for healing, stop sinning, and offer sacrifices at the Temple. Then one is ready to "give the physician his place" (38:12). Nevertheless, the physician too has been created by God and is an instrument of God. Indeed, the physician has an obligation to pray to God that he might make the right diagnosis and have success in healing people (38:13-14).

Ben Sira goes so far as to equate sinning against God and defying the physician (38:15), precisely because they work together in a kind of synergy. According to Ben Sira there is no separation between medicine and religion.

Social Relations

Humans are by nature social beings. They talk together, eat together, make financial arrangements together, and find happiness together. For all these social relationships Ben Sira provides wise advice, and he gives special prominence to the values of wisdom and fear of the Lord in guiding all aspects of everyday social life. (For his treatment of friendship see the next chapter.)

Topic 1: Speech (5:9–6:1; 18:15-29; 19:4-17; 20:1-8, 18-23; 23:7-15; 27:4-7, 11-15; 28:8-26). For most people speech is the most common vehicle used in relating to others. Since scribes/sages lived by their wits and words, it is easy to understand why Ben Sira gave so much attention to this topic.[4] Moreover, he lived in an oral culture, and those who could speak persuasively and wisely would be especially honored by their peers. In the midst of Ben Sira's opening reflections on honor and shame in 4:20–6:4 he stresses the need for truthful speech ("wisdom becomes known through speech," 4:24), affirms that "honor and dishonor come from speaking" (5:13), and criticizes vehemently the "double-tongued" (5:14).

The central chapters in Sirach give great attention to various aspects of speech. In 18:15-29 Ben Sira observes that pleasant and gracious speech is better than any good gift (18:15-18), and reminds us that "those who are skilled in words become wise themselves" (18:29). In 19:4-17 he warns against spreading gossip about others and giving easy credence to gossip heard from others.

After reflecting on the uses and misuses of silence in 20:1-8 Ben Sira observes that "a slip on the pavement is better than a slip of the tongue" (20:18) and that "a lie is an ugly blot on a person" (20:24). The passage with the heading "Discipline of the Tongue" in the Greek manuscript tradition (23:7-15) is concerned primarily with sins of speech: inappropriate oaths, blasphemy, vulgar language, and abusive speech. In 27:4-7 Ben Sira proposes that "a person's speech discloses the cultivation of his mind," and so speech can provide the most accurate criterion for judging a person. In 27:11-15 he contrasts the speech of the wise and that of fools. Finally, in 28:8-26 he reflects at length on the destructive effects of bad speech and urges that the utmost caution and prudence be used before speaking: "make a door and a bolt for your mouth" (28:25).

---

[4] See John Okoye, *Speech in Ben Sira with Special Reference to 5,9–6,1* (Frankfurt: Peter Lang, 1995).

Topic 2: Manners and Moderation (31:12–32:13; 37:27-31). Ben Sira's wisdom teachings are often very practical. At his school he was training young men to become public persons of high repute, and so his instructions touched even on proper table manners and moderate consumption of food and drink. His basic principle is "in everything you do be moderate" (31:22).

Ben Sira's practical advice on these matters is aimed primarily at young men hoping to move up in their social world. He is especially concerned to warn them about words and deeds that might bring upon them disgrace and shame. By exercising moderation and avoiding excessive attention in public the prospective sage will increase the likelihood of greater honor or at least do nothing to stand in its way.

In the instruction about table manners (31:12-18) the major concern is not drawing negative attention to oneself through uncouth or obnoxious behavior. There are certain things a sage should not say, such as blurting out "How much food there is here!" (31:12), or do, such as reaching for everything in sight, crowding one's neighbors to get at the food, or being first in line to get food. Rather, the sage should eat and behave like a well brought up person, and even be the first to stop eating (presumably to exhibit self-control). The basic principle is to show sensitivity toward one's neighbors ("in every matter be thoughtful," 31:15), with the result that such moderate behavior might contribute to one's reputation as a wise and disciplined person. This advice presupposes that the sage travels in a prosperous and status-conscious segment of society where good and bad table manners might noticed and evaluated.

With regard to consuming food (31:19-24) and drink (31:25-31) Ben Sira insists on moderation. He warns that excessive consumption of either may lead to bad physical health and even death, whereas moderation in their use will bring with it good health and sound sleep. While recognizing that excessive drinking of wine may bring one to a physical breakdown or lead one to start quarrels, Ben Sira allows that in moderation drinking wine may have good effects: "Wine is very life to humans beings if taken in moderation" (31:27).

When a sage is appointed to act as "master of the feast" (the person who arranges and presides over the banquet), according to 32:1-2 he should be primarily concerned for the guests and not act in an overbearing and overly conspicuous manner. If the sage is an old man (32:3-6) he should not speak so loudly as to drown out the sound of the music. If he is young (32:7-10) he should speak seldom and then only briefly, being careful not to draw excessive attention to himself. And according to 32:11-13 the sage should not be the last to leave the party. Rather, it is better that he go home relatively early and enjoy himself there without excessive boasting. And the evening should end with a prayer of thanksgiving: "But above all, bless your Maker, who fills you with his good gifts" (32:13).

One last piece of advice about moderation in eating appears in 37:27-31. After general comments on testing what is good for you and what you enjoy, Ben Sira warns: "Do not be greedy for every delicacy, and do not eat without restraint" (37:29). In particular he observes that gluttony can and does bring sickness and even death.

Topic 3: Money and Property (3:30–4:10; 29:1-28). Ben Sira lived in an agrarian society, one that depended in large part on agriculture and related enterprises. In this society wealth and property were not evenly distributed, but were mainly in the hands of a small group of wealthy persons at the top of the economic pyramid. Most of the population constituted the very large bottom of the pyramid, with a relatively small number functioning as mediators between the wealthy few and the mass of workers. Ben Sira himself and his students may be classified among the mediators or retainers, who by their intelligence and charm brokered arrangements between rich and poor. All these people lived in a "limited good" society, where the motto was not "There's always more where that came from" but rather "That's all there is," and so we must compete for our share.

Against this background Ben Sira's attitude is both generous and practical. His basic position is summed up in 29:20: "Assist your neighbor to the best of your ability, but be careful not to fall yourself." In 29:1-28 he treats borrowing and lending (29:1-7), almsgiving (29:8-13; see also 3:30–4:10), guaranteeing the debts of others (29:14-20), and the necessity of preserving financial independence (29:21-28). He expects that his students will be involved in financial dealings and seeks to provide them with wise guidance in keeping with their religious ideals.

In 29:1-7 Ben Sira treats the topic of loans from the double perspective of lender and borrower. In 29:1-3 he encourages making loans as an act of mercy in accord with God's commandments in the Torah (Exod 22:25; Lev 25:35-37; etc.), which meant forgoing one's right to interest on the loan. If one is the recipient of a loan, the loan should be repaid on time, if for no other reason than that those who deal honestly with lenders tend to get more loans in the future. On the contrary, those who fail to observe the terms of loans make themselves a nuisance (29:4-7). Some even seem to regard a loan as a windfall, and the result of their dishonesty is that "many refuse to lend . . . from fear of being defrauded needlessly" (29:7).

In a society with many poor persons and without an organized "welfare" system, almsgiving was necessary for the public good and was expected from those with money, honor, and high religious principles. Again Ben Sira in 29:8-13 reminds his readers that the commandment to give alms appears in the Torah: "do not be hard-hearted or tight-fisted toward your needy neighbor" (Deut 15:7). He promises that almsgiving will build up a spiritual treasure more profitable than gold and will rescue the giver from disasters and enemies. Back in 3:30–4:10 Ben Sira recommended almsgiving as way of atoning for sins and issued a series of "do not" sayings that reinforce the obligation of pious persons to give alms to the poor: "Do not reject a suppliant in distress, and turn your face away from the poor" (4:4).

In 29:14 Ben Sira declares that "a good person will be surety for his neighbor, but one who has lost all sense of shame will fail him." The practice of providing surety or collateral for another person's loan is criticized repeatedly in the book of Proverbs (6:1-5; 11:15; 17:18; 20:16; 22:26-27; 27:13). The dangers of doing so are obvious: "To guarantee loans from a stranger brings trouble" (Prov 11:15). While not condemning the practice, Ben Sira does criticize as shameless and sinful those who default on their loans and leave their benefactors liable to repay them. And he warns those who agree to such arrangements to "be careful not to fall yourself" (29:20).

Leviticus 25:35 allows one who has fallen into financial difficulties to become dependent on a relative, but in Sir 29:21-28 Ben Sira points out the personal and social disadvantages of availing oneself of this right. According to him it is better to live and eat in the most modest circumstances of one's own than to become dependent on someone else as a "guest." Being a guest in another's household means deferring to and even serving the "host," and living in constant fear of being turned away from his household in favor of more distinguished company.

Topic 4: Happiness (25:1-11; 30:14-25; 40:18-27). The goal of human existence for most people is generally described in terms of "happiness." But defining happiness is not so easy. Rather than dealing in abstractions, Ben Sira in 25:1-11; 30:14-25; and 40:18-27 points to some things that should make people truly happy. But, of course, for him the way to real happiness is through wisdom and fear of the Lord.

In 25:1 Ben Sira lists three sights that give pleasure: "agreement among brothers and sisters, friendship among neighbors, and a wife and a husband who live in harmony." We can presume that Ben Sira also wished for harmonious social relations in his own life. In 25:7-11 he uses a numerical proverb to generate a list of ten things that make people happy. The list underscores the importance of harmonious family and social relations and reaches its climax in 25:10: "How great is the one who finds wisdom! But none is superior to the one who fears the Lord."

In 30:14-25 Ben Sira writes about the happiness that comes from physical health, good food, and a good disposition, respectively. He ends with the practical observation that "those who are cheerful and merry at table will benefit from their food" (30:25). And in 40:18-27 Ben Sira presents a list of some things that are "good" and other things that are even "better." The good things include wealth and wages, children and building a city, cattle and orchards, wine and music, the flute and harp, grace and beauty, friends, relatives, and helpers, gold and silver, and riches and strength. The ten "better" things are finding a treasure, finding wisdom, a blameless wife, love of friends, a pleasant voice, green shoots of grain, a sensible wife, almsgiving, good counsel, and fear of the Lord. In fact, fear of the Lord really covers the whole list, since with it there is "no want" and "no need to seek for help" (40:26).

Conclusion

Ben Sira was indeed a man of his time and place (early-second-century Palestine). In matters such as patriarchy and slavery he seems to have accepted without much reflection or criticism some now dubious assumptions of his contemporaries in the land of Israel and elsewhere in the Mediterranean world. Moreover, however much we may admire the wisdom of Ben Sira we must also acknowledge some "blind spots" in his personal outlook. His misogyny sometimes reaches the level of pathology, and his male self-centeredness often seems hopelessly insensitive to the needs and happiness of others (women, children, and slaves).

But that is not the whole story. While Ben Sira frequently raises concerns about honor and shame, he does try to move his pupils to give more attention to conducting their lives against the horizon of divine wisdom and fear of the Lord. And he places the sage or scribe at the top of the social hierarchy and insists that rulers should be wise. His ideal society would exalt the values of wisdom and fear of the Lord over those of family pedigree or wealth and would place those who prove to be wise in the most prominent positions.

CHAPTER SIX

Ben Sira's Abiding Wisdom

Ben Sira's book is obviously the product of his own education as a sage and of his years of training scribes at his school in Jerusalem. It is safe to assume that the book was the product of his old age.[1] He may have written it as a "textbook." Or perhaps he regarded it as a personal synthesis of what he had learned and taught over the course of his career.[2]

The literary structure of the book of Sirach has always been something of a mystery. Most ancient wisdom books were anthologies, and maybe that was all Ben Sira intended to produce. However, it is possible that the seven major texts about wisdom (1:1-10; 4:11-19; 6:18-37; 14:20–15:10; 24:1-34; 32:14–33:6; 38:24–39:11) serve as introductions to separate cycles of his wisdom teachings, capped off with the long reflection on God's wisdom and glory made manifest in creation and in Israel's history (42:15–50:24) that functions as the grand climax of the book. These cycles may in turn reflect different "course units" or "lecture series" that Ben Sira offered in his wisdom school.[3]

Thus far most of our attention has been given to the general historical, literary, and sociocultural dimensions of book of Sirach. But what was most important to Ben Sira himself was the content of the wisdom teachings he presented in his book. While these wisdom teachings were forged in the setting of the school for scribes/sages he conducted in Jerusalem, by putting them in the form of a very large book Ben Sira sought to reach beyond the

---

[1] D. S. Williams, "The Date of Ecclesiasticus," *VT* 44 (1994) 563–66, estimates that Ben Sira wrote his book when he was about sixty years of age and his grandson (the translator) was an infant.

[2] Wolfgang Roth, "Sirach: The First Graded Curriculum," *TBT* 29 (1991) 298–302.

[3] J. D. Harvey, "Toward a Degree of Order in Ben Sira's Book," *ZAW* 105 (1993) 52–62.

confines of his own school. He stated his purpose well when he wrote: "Observe that I have not labored for myself alone, but for all who seek wisdom" (24:34).

What Ben Sira produced can be described as a handbook for personal and spiritual formation.[4] His varied, artistic, and generally interesting ways of teaching help to convey his message. His emphasis on the search for wisdom and on fear of the Lord gives spiritual depth to his teachings. Much of his practical advice is still valid, or at least worth considering. Perhaps Ben Sira's greatest achievement was his ability to integrate the common ancient Near Eastern wisdom teachings and the various strands of biblical piety (wisdom, creation, history, worship, Torah, prophecy). His recognition that creation and Israel's history show forth the glory of God is a wonderful way of looking at the world and our place within it. After 2,200 years we can still learn much about personal and spiritual formation from the book of Sirach.

Recent study of the ancient Greek and Roman philosophers has emphasized the intention of the various masters (Socrates, Plato, Aristotle, etc.) to inculcate the vision of their philosophies as a way of life. A pioneer in this line of research, Pierre Hadot, states: "such wisdom does not consist in the possession of information about reality. Instead, it too is a way of life, which corresponds to the highest activity which human beings can engage in and which is linked intentionally to the excellence and virtue of the soul."[5] While Ben Sira was not necessarily the same kind of "lover of wisdom" as Plato and Aristotle were, he certainly meant his handbook to describe a way of life.

An essential element in ancient philosophy, according to Hadot, was the practice of "spiritual exercises." Many people today know that term from the "Spiritual Exercises" of Ignatius of Loyola, the founder of the Jesuits. In the sixteenth century Ignatius developed a handbook of meditations and related instructions designed to lead "exercitants" through a highly structured program of religious formation aimed at finding God's will for them and making a decision about a state in life or some other major matter. However, Ignatius did not invent the concept of "spiritual exercises." Rather, he seems to have been working out of an ancient and respected tradition of spiritual exercises in philosophy that had also become part of the Christian tradition.

[4] Daniel J. Harrington, "Ben Sira as a Spiritual Master," *Journal of Spiritual Formation* 15 (1994) 147–57.

[5] Pierre Hadot, *What Is Ancient Philosophy?* (Cambridge: Harvard University Press, 2002) 222. See also his *Philosophy as a Way of Life: Spiritual Exercises from Socrates to Foucault* (Oxford: Blackwell, 1995).

The ten units that follow apply the concept of "spiritual exercises" to texts from the book of Sirach and related early Jewish and Christian wisdom texts. These presentations should be regarded as illustrative of an approach, not as exhaustive summaries of all the pertinent evidence on the various topics. Each exercise contains a title, a focal quotation from Sirach, a brief introduction, a synthesis of what Ben Sira has to say on the issue, a survey of other ancient approaches to that issue found mainly in the other wisdom books described in Chapter 2, and some questions for reflection and/or discussion.

The "Interfaces" between Ben Sira and the other authors are intended to highlight both their similarities and their distinctive approaches. The texts treated in these sections include not only Jewish and early Christian wisdom books but also other writings ranging from the Dead Sea scrolls to the New Testament and even Aristotle. The material there is quite diverse and can only be treated briefly. But its very diversity will contribute to our better recognizing Ben Sira's distinctive perspectives and better appreciating the options that were available in antiquity regarding major philosophical and theological issues.

These spiritual exercises seek to reproduce in some way what I imagine must have gone on in Ben Sira's school. While memorization surely played a major role in Ben Sira's pedagogy (see Chapter 4), there must have been some room for questioning, discussion, clarification, rebuttal, and assimilation on the part of his students. The texts treated in these exercises are meant as a starting point for the reader's own reflection and discussion. They provide information about Ben Sira's views and those of the other wisdom writers, but the real goal of these exercises (in accord with Ben Sira's own goal) is more "formation" than "information."

The concluding questions try to stimulate active thinking, which in turn might lead to practice. They are meant to raise questions such as these: Have you understood what Ben Sira and the other writers were talking about? Is what Ben Sira and the others say true to your experience? Why or why not? Should what they say cause you to change your thinking and/or way of living? The classical term for this activity is "meditation." It may in turn lead to the pleasure of understanding the ideas of another age, a decision to change something in your life now, and/or to pray by way of petition or thanksgiving. This kind of activity—"spiritual exercises"—will make a reality out of Ben Sira's own claim to have labored "for all who seek wisdom" (24:34).

Exercise 1: The Origin and Nature of Wisdom (Key Texts in Sirach—1:1-10; 24:1-34; 38:24–39:11). "All wisdom is from the Lord, and with him it remains forever" (1:1).

Where does wisdom come from? What is wisdom? These are questions that humans frequently ask. But few seem to work through them to arrive at satisfying answers. In a real sense the entire book known as the "Wisdom of Ben Sira" is devoted to answering those questions. For Ben Sira, what is contained in his book constitutes true wisdom.

Ben Sira: Where wisdom comes from is the topic of the first lines of instruction in Ben Sira's book (1:1-10). His answer is that all wisdom is from God, and all wisdom remains with God forever (1:1).[6] His opening poem in praise of wisdom focuses first on God (1:1-3), then on wisdom (1:4, 6), and then again on God (1:8-10). It affirms that there are many things beyond human comprehension: the number of the sands of the sea, of the drops of rain, and so on. Only God knows those things. Wisdom is a creation of God, and only God knows all the subtleties of wisdom. From the start Ben Sira, following the tradition of Proverbs 8, endows Wisdom with personal (feminine) characteristics (see 1:4).[7] Only the Lord is truly and completely wise (1:8). The wisdom God makes available to humans is not only a creation from God but also a gift from God. The origin of all wisdom, according to Ben Sira, is God.

The "Praise of Wisdom" in 24:1-34 is the approximate center of Ben Sira's book, and in a real sense it constitutes the heart of his book. Here Wisdom personified in feminine terms speaks in the heavenly court (24:1-2). In 24:3-7 Wisdom recounts her creation from the "mouth of the Most High" and her search for a home or resting place within creation. Then in 24:8-12 she tells how God chose for her a dwelling place in the Temple at Jerusalem: "In the holy tent I ministered before him, and so I was established in Zion" (24:10). Then, with a series of "tree" comparisons ("like a cedar . . . cypress . . . palm tree") in 24:13-17, Wisdom calls attention to her attractiveness and power to give abundant life. Finally in 24:19-22 Wisdom issues an invitation to come to her banquet: "Come to me, you who desire me, and eat your fill of my fruits" (24:19). The fruits of Wisdom include not only knowledge but also the ability to avoid shame and even sin: "Whoever obeys me will not be put to shame, and those who work with me will not sin" (24:22).

The boldest and most original theological move in the book of Sirach appears in 24:23, when Ben Sira identifies Wisdom and the Torah: "All this is the book of the covenant of the Most High God, the law that Moses commanded us as an inheritance for the congregation of Jacob." For Ben Sira

---

[6] See Renate Egger-Wenzel, ed., *Ben Sira's God.* BZAW 321 (Berlin: de Gruyter, 2001).

[7] See Claudia Camp, *Wisdom and the Feminine in the Book of Proverbs* (Sheffield: Almond, 1985); and Celia M. Deutsch, *Lady Wisdom, Jesus, and the Sages: Metaphor and Social Context in Matthew's Gospel* (Harrisburg, PA: Trinity Press International, 1997).

the essence of divine wisdom is to be found in the law of Moses. His claim is that the Torah is true Wisdom, and Wisdom dwells in the Temple. The Torah serves to reveal God's own wisdom, and Wisdom is present in the rituals of sacrifice and prayer conducted in the Jerusalem Temple. For Ben Sira there was no conflict between the traditional wisdom of the ancient Near East (what we might call philosophy or secular wisdom) and the Torah and the rituals conducted in the Jerusalem Temple (what we might call religious wisdom). Indeed, Ben Sira's great theological and intellectual contribution was to bring these apparently disparate entities into harmony and even unity.

In this way Ben Sira joins the ancient Near Eastern wisdom tradition to the distinctive religious traditions and institutions of ancient Israel. Thus he integrates human wisdom and divine wisdom, and celebrates the God of Israel as the origin and source of all wisdom. And that wisdom is super-abundant, as the comparisons with six great rivers in 24:25-27 show: "It overflows like the Phishon with wisdom, and like the Tigris at the time of the first fruits" (24:25). In this context Ben Sira the teacher of wisdom likens himself to "a canal from a river, like a water channel into a garden" (24:30).

For certain persons to receive the gift of wisdom more fully and to make the best use of it for themselves and others it was necessary to get a proper "scribal" education. Ben Sira conducted a school for "scribes." His scribes not only learned the basics of reading and writing, but also developed the theoretical knowledge and practical skills that would equip them to serve as leaders and counselors on the wider stage of society and history.

In 38:24-34a Ben Sira reminds us that education demands a certain amount of "leisure." Indeed, the word "scholar" and related terms derive from the Greek *scholē,* meaning "leisure." And "liberal" in the expressions "liberal arts" and "liberal education" evokes the ancient Roman ideal of the education befitting "free men" *(liberi)* as opposed to slaves or craftsmen. While they are vital and necessary to the good of their society, neither the farmer, artisan, smith, nor potter had the leisure and so the opportunity to pursue the "scholarly" or "liberal" training that went on in Ben Sira's school for young sages.

In 38:34b–39:4 Ben Sira gives a glimpse of the curriculum in his academy. Central to its program was "the study of the law of the Most High," but it also included other resources such as "the wisdom of all the ancients . . . prophecies . . . the sayings of the famous . . . the subtleties of parables . . . the hidden meaning of proverbs" (39:1-3). It also involved contact with important persons ("the great . . . rulers") and travel in foreign lands as important helps toward learning "what is good and evil in the human lot" (39:4).

Study at Ben Sira's school was animated and guided by prayer. Since "all wisdom is from God" (1:1) and God is "the one who is wise" (1:8), it seems fitting and necessary that those who seek for wisdom should ask God for the gift of wisdom. And so in 39:5-8 Ben Sira directs that the search for wisdom at his school be carried out in an atmosphere of prayer.

One of the results of acquiring the wisdom taught at Ben Sira's school will be a good "name," by which the sage will honored during life and re-membered after death (39:9-11). Indeed, for Ben Sira a good name is the most lasting form of honor and the most certain form of immortality: "Many will praise his understanding; it will never be blotted out" (39:9).

Interfaces: Ben Sira was quite optimistic about wisdom. He was sure that we can know much about God and human existence, and he wrote his book to convey what he had learned. He knew what wisdom is (from the Torah, the wisdom of the ancients, practical human experience, etc.) and where it was to be found (at the Jerusalem Temple). By contrast, Qoheleth claims to know very little about wisdom. He admits that "wisdom exceeds folly as light exceeds darkness" (2:13). But he goes on to observe that the same fate—death—awaits both the sage and the fool (2:14-16), and that even the search for wisdom is "vanity and a chasing after wind" (2:17). The fundamental problem is that while all wisdom may be from God, human beings do not seem able to gain access to it: "even though those who are wise claim to know, they cannot find it out" (8:17).

The skepticism shown by Qoheleth is not at all typical of ancient Jewish wisdom teachers. In fact, two of their pursuits were trying to answer the questions, What is wisdom? and Where is wisdom to be found? A key text in this debate is Prov 8:22-31, a poem in which Wisdom speaks for herself in a fe-male *persona*. Whether her female character depends on Hebrew grammar (*hokma* is a feminine noun) or some statement is being made to counter the female deities of other religions (Asherah, Isis), Wisdom describes her com-ing into being at the very moment of God's creating all things: "The Lord cre-ated me at the beginning of his work" (8:22). She claims not only to have been present at creation but also to continue God's work throughout history: "then I was beside him, like a master worker" (8:30). Wisdom is said to rejoice in the inhabited world and to delight in the human race (8:31).

Proverbs 8:22-31 provided the framework for Ben Sira's praise of Wis-dom in Sirach 24. It also introduced the theme of Wisdom's search for a dwelling place on earth. Of course, Ben Sira identifies Wisdom's dwelling place as the Jerusalem Temple ("in the holy tent . . . in Zion," 24:10). And he identifies the Law of Moses as the content of wisdom: "All this is the book of the covenant of the Most High God, the law that Moses commanded" (24:23).

The nature and dwelling place of Wisdom are also major concerns in the Wisdom of Solomon. For this first-century B.C.E. Jewish author based in Alexandria in Egypt, Wisdom is what the Greek philosophers regarded as the "world soul": "the spirit of the Lord has filled the world, and that which holds all things together knows what is said" (1:7). The spirit that is in Wisdom is said to be "intelligent, holy, unique, manifold, subtle, mobile, clear, unpolluted . . ." (7:23). She is described as "a pure emanation of the glory of the Almighty . . . a reflection of eternal light, a spotless mirror of the working of God, and an image of his goodness" (7:25-26). In this perspective Wisdom is everywhere and in everything, and all creation is a reflection of the Wisdom of God.

A very different approach appears in *1 Enoch* 42, part of the "Book of Parables (or Similitudes)" in *1 Enoch* 37–71. As in Proverbs 8, Sirach 24, and the Wisdom of Solomon, Wisdom is a female figure present with God in heaven. But when Wisdom goes forth in search of a dwelling place on earth she finds none, and so she returns to her place in heaven: "Then Wisdom went out to dwell with the children of the people, but she found no dwelling place. So Wisdom returned to her place, and she settled permanently among the angels" (42:2). That means that when humans want to obtain real wisdom they must take a heavenly journey in a dream, a vision, or some other esoteric experience. The books associated with Enoch purport to describe such experiences and the wisdom conveyed in them.

Early Christians developed their distinctive approach to wisdom in terms of Jesus. In what is generally regarded as an early Christian hymn preserved in Col 1:15-20, Jesus is described in terms of the Jewish texts about the figure of Wisdom: "He is the image of the invisible God, the firstborn of all creation; for in him all things in heaven and on earth were created . . . . He himself is before all things, and in him all things hold together." In this perspective Jesus is the Wisdom of God. And Wisdom now resides in him and in the church as the body of Christ: "in him all the fullness of God was pleased to dwell" (1:19). For other examples of Wisdom christology see John 1:1-18 and Heb 1:3.

These early Jewish and Christian texts represent a wide variety of approaches to the nature of wisdom and where wisdom is to be found. For Ben Sira wisdom is the Torah and dwells in the Jerusalem Temple. According to the Wisdom of Solomon, wisdom is the world soul animating all creation and so is to be found everywhere and in everything. In *1 Enoch* 42 wisdom remains a heavenly figure not at home on earth and is accessible only through dreams, visions, and reports about such experiences. For Christians, Jesus is the wisdom of God, and he is present in "the body of Christ," which is the church.

Questions: (1) How do you define wisdom? (2) Where do you find wisdom? (3) What do you see as the strengths and weaknesses of Ben Sira's approach? (4) Which approach among the several discussed here do you find the most satisfying? (5) How do you explain the choice of female characteristics in the descriptions of the figure of wisdom?

Exercise 2: Fear of the Lord (Key Texts in Sirach—1:11-20; 2:1-18; 34:14-20). "The fear of the Lord is glory and exultation, and gladness and a crown for rejoicing" (1:11).

To many people the expression "fear of the Lord" carries very negative connotations. It often evokes stereotyped (and wrong) images of the wrathful God of the Old Testament. However, things seem to have gone in the opposite direction in recent years. In describing her own religious formation, one Catholic-educated "Gen-Xer" (Generation X refers to someone raised in the 1980s or early 1990s) observed that "I was never taught that I needed to 'fear the Lord.'" Ben Sira (and many biblical writers) would surely declare her religious education to be seriously deficient.

Ben Sira: In the biblical context the "fear of the Lord" refers to the respect, gratitude, and way of life that are owed to God the "awesome one" in response to the gift of life and the revelation of God's wisdom. It describes the subjective response to the objective experience of God. Rudolf Otto termed the experience of God *mysterium tremendum et fascinans* ("the mystery that both frightens and fascinates"). Otto's words provide a good description of what Ben Sira and the other biblical writers meant by the "fear of the Lord." It is both awesome and disturbing.

For Ben Sira "fear of the Lord" was not a negative concept. Immediately after describing the origin and nature of wisdom in 1:1-10 he offers a reflection in 1:11-20 on fear of the Lord as the proper response to God's gift of Wisdom. He first insists in 1:11-13 that fear of the Lord is an occasion for joy: "The fear of the Lord is glory and exultation, and gladness and a crown of rejoicing." Then he proclaims in 1:14-20 that fearing the Lord is the beginning of wisdom (1:14-15), the fullness of wisdom (1:16-17), the crown of wisdom (1:18-19), and the root of wisdom (1:20). Without proper respect and awe before God it is impossible to receive the wisdom of God and to live in accord with it.

However, the fear of the Lord does not exempt one from testing and suffering. Indeed, in 2:1-18 Ben Sira instructs his students to expect suffering: "My child, when you come to serve the Lord, prepare yourself for testing" (2:1). With this opening Ben Sira places the suffering his students will surely undergo in the category of "discipline" or "instruction." Just as athletes, musicians, and artists must practice constantly and work very hard to learn their crafts, so those who seek wisdom must do the same. Ben Sira makes this point with the common biblical analogy of gold being "tested in the fire" (2:5). In the midst of such testing, the proper attitude of those who fear the Lord is to hope and trust in God: "Wait for his mercy . . . trust in him . . . hope for good things" (2:7-9). What sustains those who fear the Lord is the biblical understanding of God as the merciful one: "For the Lord is compassionate and merciful; he forgives sins and saves in time of distress" (2:11). They love the Lord and keep his law: "Those who fear the Lord seek to please him, and those who love him are filled with his law" (2:16). For Ben Sira fear of the Lord, love for God, and keeping the Lord's commandments all belong together. They are not opposites or contradictory. The God he worships and serves is the Merciful One (2:11, 16).

By placing these reflections on fear of the Lord early in his book and repeating the term frequently Ben Sira gives special prominence to the theme and makes "fear of the Lord" the context or framework for all the instructions in the rest of the book. However, in 34:14-20 there is still another explicit treatment: "Happy is the soul that fears the Lord" (34:17). This attitude gives one life, hope, and courage in everyday life. Those who fear the Lord love the Lord and experience God as "a mighty shield and strong support, a shelter from scorching wind and a shade from noonday sun, a guard against stumbling and a help against falling" (37:19). In fact, fear of the Lord contributes to both spiritual and physical health: "He lifts up the soul and makes the eyes sparkle" (37:20).

Interfaces: The theme of fear of the Lord appears at the end of the book of Qoheleth, though there is a dispute whether it has been inserted there by a later editor who was trying to bring this peculiar book into line with more conventional Jewish piety. At any rate, someone—whether it was Qoheleth or a later scribe—offered "fear of the Lord" as a summary of the entire book: "Fear God, and keep his commandments; for that is the whole duty of everyone" (12:13).

Fear of the Lord is a key concept in other biblical wisdom literature. In Prov 2:5 the instructor promises that those who seek consistently after wisdom "will understand the fear of the Lord and find the knowledge of God." Likewise, the wonderful poem in Job 28 on how hard it is for humans to find wisdom ends by observing that "the fear of the Lord, that is wisdom; and to depart from evil is understanding" (28:28).

In the New Testament the life of Jesus is bracketed by references to what can be called "holy fear." At the announcement of Jesus' birth Mary is initially perplexed and frightened but is reassured by the angel Gabriel: "Do not be afraid, Mary, for your have found favor with God" (Luke 1:30). Likewise, when the women followers of Jesus find his tomb empty on Easter

Sunday and are told that "he has been raised," Mark tells us that "terror and amazement had seized them" (16:8). While both texts allude to the more primitive sense of fear, they also evoke by their context in the gospels the sense of awe and reverence associated with "fear" in the biblical wisdom writings. And immediately after the early Christian hymn about Jesus' pre-existence, incarnation, death, resurrection, and exaltation in Phil 2:6-11, Paul in 2:12 directs Christians to "work out your salvation with fear and trembling." Any religious education program that neglects fear of the Lord is not faithful to the biblical tradition and does a disservice to its participants.

Questions: (1) Was "fear of the Lord" part of your religious formation? (2) In light of the texts from Ben Sira and other writers, has your understanding of "fear of the Lord" changed? (3) Is there some other term that might better express the biblical concept of fear of the Lord? (4) Do you ever regard suffering as a "discipline"? (5) Are Ben Sira's promises to those who fear the Lord realistic or empty?

Exercise 3: The Quest for Wisdom (Key Texts in Sirach—4:11-19; 6:18-37; 14:20–15:10; 51:13-30). "Whoever loves her [Wisdom] loves life, and those who seek her from early morning are filled with joy" (4:12).

There are three fundamental questions every person should address in life: Who am I? What is my goal in life? And how do I reach that goal? These three questions provide the framework in which thoughtful people live their lives, and they supply the horizon against which the ancient wisdom teachers and Ben Sira in particular lived and worked.

Ben Sira: In the series of texts about the origin and nature of wisdom Ben Sira taught that wisdom is a gift from God and embraces both practical reflection on human experience (traditional wisdom) and divine revelation (Torah). In the passage about fear of the Lord, Ben Sira identified the proper attitude humans should have in the face of their encounter with God and the gift of wisdom. Both sets of texts emphasize that finding wisdom demands an active quest on the part of the human person. Wisdom does not simply fall into one's lap. It involves a quest. That quest entails searching and discipline but results in great rewards, especially happiness (which is what all humans seek). The texts treated in this unit all evoke the great themes of the quest for wisdom: search, discipline, and rewards.

In 4:11-19 Ben Sira reflects on how wisdom herself aids those who seek her to achieve their goal: "Wisdom teaches her children and gives help to those who seek her" (4:11). Those rewards include a full life, joy, glory, blessings from God, and God's love (4:12-14). The idea is that those who seek and find wisdom attain the goal toward which all humans strive (happiness) as part of the process, as a kind of byproduct of the quest for wisdom. In 4:15-16 Ben Sira further promises that those who obey wisdom will be important within human affairs ("will judge the nations") and live in security, and that they and their descendants will possess wisdom— provided they remain faithful to the quest for wisdom. In 4:17-19 Ben Sira warns that the quest for wisdom demands testing and self-discipline, "for at first she will walk with them on tortuous paths" (4:17). He reminds his students that if they go astray "she will forsake them and hand them over to their ruin" (4:19).

The theme of discipline as the way to wisdom is developed at greater length in 6:18-37. The passage consists of three units (6:18-22, 23-31, 32-37), each beginning with the address "my child" (literally, "my son"). In 6:18-22 Ben Sira reminds all seekers after wisdom that the quest necessarily involves discipline, but he also promises that those who accept wisdom's discipline will receive her rewards. In making his positive point Ben Sira compares the seeker to a farmer who plants seeds and cultivates the soil, waits patiently and eventually gets "a good harvest." In a related warning he observes that the discipline required in the quest for wisdom "seems very harsh to the undisciplined" (6:20) and will be "like a heavy stone" to fools (6:21).

The second "my child" instruction (6:23-31) uses the imagery of the "yoke" or harness placed on beasts of burden. Ben Sira urges his pupils to accept the yoke of discipline: "Put your feet into her fetters, and your neck into her collar" (6:24). The "yoke" presumably includes the curriculum taught in Ben Sira's wisdom school and the way of righteous living that goes along with it. Those who take upon themselves the yoke of wisdom are promised rest and joy (6:28). Indeed, as they make progress in their search for wisdom, according to 6:29-30, the various parts of the harness will turn into rewards or even benefits: Fetters become a strong defense, the collar becomes a glorious robe, the yoke becomes a golden ornament, and the bonds become a purple cord. Indeed, those who accept the discipline required in the quest for wisdom "will wear her like a glorious robe, and put her on like a splendid crown" (6:31).

The third "my child" instruction (6:32-37) spells out two important elements in the quest for wisdom: willingness to learn from people wiser than oneself (6:33-36), and applying oneself to the divine revelation contained in Israel's Scriptures (6:37). These are essential aspects of the discipline required to obtain wisdom. Ben Sira advises his students to listen to what wise persons have to say and to seek out mentors who may help them on their way to wisdom: "Who is wise? Attach yourself to such a one" (6:34). But it is also important to apply oneself to the study and practice of the "statutes of the Lord " (6:37), since God is the origin of all wisdom and can bring the quest for wisdom to its goal of happiness.

For many philosophers the goal or "end" *(finis)* of human existence is "happiness" *(beatitudo* in Latin). The "beatitude" form that is so frequent in ancient wisdom writings serves to designate certain persons and behaviors as reaching the goal of happiness. In 14:20-27 Ben Sira makes his contribution to this conversation when he declares: "Happy is the person who meditates on wisdom and reasons intelligently" (14:20). In 14:22-27 he goes on to describe the search for wisdom and happiness in terms of three sets of images: hunting (14:22), camping out at a lover's house (14:23-25), and shade and shelter from a tree (14:26-27).

In 15:1 Ben Sira summarizes his whole theological outlook in one sentence: "Whoever fears the Lord will do this, and whoever holds to the law will obtain wisdom." This statement links his three favorite theological concepts: fear of the Lord, the law, and wisdom. The accompanying instruction (15:2-10) focuses on the benefits of the quest for wisdom. In 15:2-6 he portrays wisdom as coming to the seeker "like a mother and like a young bride" who provides nurture, support, honor, joy, and "an everlasting name." This praise of wisdom's benefits is balanced by a warning in 15:7-10 that "the foolish will not obtain her, and sinners will not see her."

In his "autobiographical"poem in 51:13-30 Ben Sira describes his own quest for wisdom. In 51:13-17 he claims that his search began with prayer ("I sought wisdom openly in my prayer"), involved appropriate behavior ("my foot walked on straight paths"), and demanded the discipline of study ("I found for myself much instruction"). As he made progress (see 51:18-21) Ben Sira resolved to live according to wisdom and describes his life in this way: "My soul grappled with wisdom, and in my conduct I was strict" (51:19). He also observes that his continuing quest had been marked at every stage by prayer: "I spead out my hands to the heavens . . . . I directed my soul to her" (51:19-20).

In his invitation to prospective students (51:23-30) to come to his "house of instruction" Ben Sira demands that they be willing to accept the discipline necessary to obtain wisdom: "Put you neck under her yoke" (51:26; see 6:24-26). At the same time he promises that the quest for wisdom will bring great benefits. To underline his point he cites himself as an example of those who have found happiness in the quest for wisdom: "See with your own eyes that I have labored little and found for myself much serenity" (51:27). The quest for wisdom involves a search and entails strict discipline, but it can and does issue in the "happiness" *(beatitudo)* that all humans seek.

Interfaces: Since Qoheleth regarded wisdom as beyond human grasp he naturally considered the quest for wisdom an exercise in futility. In 1:12-18 he describes his own search for wisdom: "I, the Teacher . . . applied my mind to seek and to search out by wisdom all that is done under heaven." He concluded that "it is an unhappy business that God has given human beings to be busy with" (1:13). He goes on to say that when "I applied my mind to know wisdom . . . I perceived that this also is but a chasing after wind" (1:17). Later in his book he describes his personal quest in very negative terms: "I said, 'I will be wise,' but it was far from me. That which is, is far off, and deep, very deep; who can find it out?" (7:23-24).

Likewise, in Job 28 in a poem about how hard it is for humans to find wisdom, the conclusion is that only God "understands the way to it, and he knows its place" (28:23). What is left as wisdom for humans is simply "fear of the Lord" and departing from evil. While humans can use their ingenuity to discover many things, true wisdom remains elusive for them and the quest for it seems futile.

In later forms of Second Temple Judaism the quest for wisdom takes very different forms. For the apocalyptists behind the book of Daniel and 4 Ezra the real wisdom concerns the future, and this is accessible as revelation through visions and dreams. For the "scribes and Pharisees" and the rabbis as their successors, wisdom is to be found in the study and practice of God's revelation contained in the Torah. For early Christians wisdom is to be found in the person and teachings of Jesus. According to Col 1:15-20 and John 1:1-18, Jesus is the Wisdom of God and the Word of God. What God wanted to tell humans, God told them in the person of Jesus, who is both the revealer and the revelation of God. Jesus is divine wisdom in human form.

Questions: (1) How do you obtain wisdom? (2) Is wisdom a gift, or something you achieve? (3) What kind of discipline does your search for wisdom demand? (4) What is the goal of your search for wisdom? (5) Do you ever share Qoheleth's sense of pessimism about the quest for wisdom?

Exercise 4: Some Virtues and Vices (Key Texts in Sirach—3:17-20; etc.). "The greater you are, the more you must humble yourself; so you will find favor in the sight of the Lord" (3:18).

To find wisdom and the happiness that goes with it, one must work at it. One obvious and important approach involves cultivating the virtues and avoiding the vices. Ben Sira and the other ancient wisdom teachers provide solid advice about which virtues best contribute to a life spent in the quest for wisdom and fear of the Lord.

Ben Sira: Like all teachers of wisdom, Ben Sira spends much time and energy in exhorting readers to virtuous living. Throughout his long book he refers to all kinds of virtues to be cultivated and vices to be avoided. However, there are in Sirach no systematic treatments of virtues and vices, no definitions, and no overarching principle or principles to explain the various virtues and vices. Rather, Ben Sira operates at a common-sense level with regard to the virtues and vices in ordinary life, and at a theological level in subordinating all the virtues to the supreme excellence of "the God of all."

Most of the virtues and vices mentioned by Ben Sira can be found in the writings of other ancient philosophers and wisdom teachers as well as the moralists of all ages, but one virtue that is rather distinctive to the biblical tradition is humility. In an honor-shame culture such as Ben Sira's one might not expect to find humility as a virtue to be recommended. Nevertheless, Ben Sira, like other biblical writers, promotes humility as an important virtue mainly for theological reasons.

At 3:17-20, early in his book, Ben Sira adopts the instruction format ("my child") and explains why humility can be regarded as a virtue. His reasons are thoroughly theological. The point is that those who understand who God is will be eager to humble themselves as a token of their subordination to God. In 3:17 Ben Sira urges his students to perform their tasks "with humility" ("meekness" in Greek), on the grounds that they will be loved by the very humble-lowly-poor people whom God loves. In 3:18 he notes that the "great" in this world must work especially hard in the pursuit of humility in order to find favor with God. In 3:20 Ben Sira celebrates the greatness of God and observes that "by the humble he is glorified." These verses lay the theological foundations for the biblical virtue of humility. Because God is great and all humans are lowly in comparison, and because God is best served by those who recognize the difference, in this framework it is "reasonable" to be humble and humility is an important virtue.

Among the many other virtues Ben Sira recommends, he gives special prominence to those that are appropriate to the lifelong pursuit of wisdom and a commitment to the virtuous life. To those setting out on the quest for wisdom he recommends the need for patience: "Accept whatever befalls you, and in times of humiliation be patient" (2:4). To those who are on the way to wisdom he stresses the need for being resolute: "A wooden beam firmly bonded into a building is not loosened by an earthquake, so the mind firmly resolved after due reflection will not be afraid in a crisis" (22:16). He also emphasizes the need for self-control ("Do not follow your base desires, but restrain your appetites," 18:30) and for self-care ("health and fitness are better than any gold," 30:15). These are all virtues for the long haul, for the quest for wisdom and the practice of it over a lifetime.

Many of the vices Ben Sira condemns concern the traps or obstacles one may encounter along the way to wisdom. Just as he praised the virtue of humility, so he criticizes the vice of pride and does so in a theological context: "The beginning of human pride is to forsake the Lord . . . the beginning of pride is sin" (10:12-13). Other vices that come in for particular condemnation are foul language (23:12-15; 28:12-16), giving in to sexual passion (23:16-27), betraying confidences (27:16-21), and anger and vengeance (27:30–28:11). Giving in to these vices constitutes inappropriate behavior for those who earnestly seek wisdom.

Interfaces: The most perceptive and influential philosophical analysis of virtues and vices in antiquity is found in Aristotle's *Nicomachean Ethics*. There is nothing like it in the Bible (or anywhere else). Aristotle defines virtue as a state of character that makes a person be good and act well. In investigating the virtues and vices Aristotle uses the concept of the "mean" between excess and deficiency. Both extremes are vices, and the virtue stands in the middle as the "mean." Thus modesty is a virtue while the excesses on either side—bashfulness and shamelessness—are vices; temperance is the mean between self-indulgence and excessive abstinence; and courage is the mean between (over-) confidence and fear.

Many of the virtues (and corresponding vices) Aristotle treats appear in one form or another in the ancient Jewish wisdom writings: justice, temperance, truthfulness, friendliness, prudence, and continence. In fact, the book of Wisdom depicts Wisdom herself as the teacher of the classic Greek constellation of the four cardinal virtues: "for she teaches self-control and prudence, justice and courage" (8:7). But in Proverbs or Sirach, for example, there is not much emphasis on courage, magnanimity, or pride. On the contrary, humility, faith in God, and concern with divine retribution fit well with the Jewish theological context but have little or no place in Aristotle's philosophy.

The book of Job is a full-scale exploration of the alleged relationship between sin (or vice) and divine retribution. The friends are convinced that since Job is suffering, he must therefore have sinned. In other words, they regarded his suffering as divine retribution. The point of the book, however, is to deny the alleged link between sin and suffering in the case of Job, the exemplar of virtuous living.

Qoheleth knows well the difference between virtues and vices. For example, he declares: "the patient in spirit are better than the proud in spirit" (7:8). But in the end these differences are really not very important, since death is the fate of all humans and there are no rewards and punishments after death. Therefore his advice is to enjoy the simple pleasures of life in the present, though always in moderation: "There is nothing better for mortals than to eat and drink and find enjoyment in their toil" (2:24; see 5:18).

The book of Wisdom represents an opposite approach, so much so that it may well have been written to counter the skepticism and moral relativism of Qoheleth. The author of Wisdom was convinced that at the last judgment the righteous will be vindicated and rewarded with eternal life with God for their faithful pursuit of wisdom and virtue in this life: "For though in the sight of others they were punished, their hope is full of immortality" (3:4).

Questions: (1) How do you understand and define "virtue" and "vice"? (2) Do you regard humility as a virtue? Why or why not? (3) What difference does having a religious framework make in approaching the virtues and vices? (4) What virtues do you need especially to cultivate in your life? (5) What vices do you need to avoid?

Exercise 5: Friendship (Key Texts in Sirach—6:5-17; 9:10-16; 19:13-17; 22:19-26; 27:16-21; 37:1-6). "Those who fear the Lord direct their friendship aright, for as they are, so are their neighbors" (6:17).

There was an old song that proclaimed very loudly: "You've gotta have friends." Most of us accept our need for friends. We "make friends" mainly from those we meet in our living situations, schools, neighborhoods, workplaces, and so forth. However, we may give surprisingly little thought to what real friendship involves. Do we "have" friends? Or "are" we friends? Do we collect and discard friends as if they were possessions? What is friendship? How do we "make" friends? What do we expect from friends? Whom do we call "friends"? And how and why do friendships end?

Ben Sira: The book of Sirach contains the most extensive treatment of the theme of friendship in the Bible.[8] It provides practical advice about making friends, keeping friends, and being a friend. It gives no attention to the theory or definition of friendship. Rather, it offers reflections based on human experience and holds out "friendship in the Lord" as the ideal.

In 6:5-17 Ben Sira first observes that "pleasant speech" is a good way to make friends but urges caution and testing before calling someone a true friend (6:5-7). He goes on to give examples of false friends, mainly people who enjoy the fruits of friendship in good times but turn against you or disappear in distress and trouble (6:8-13). On the contrary, true or faithful friends are a sturdy shelter, a priceless treasure, and a lifesaving medicine (6:14-16). The best source of faithful friends is the company of those who fear the Lord (6:17). Those who fear the Lord not only will be true friends but also will help you to become even more as they are.

In 9:10 Ben Sira recommends fidelity to old friends, "for new ones cannot equal them," and compares new friends to new wine and old friends to old wine. The new wine needs maturation and testing, while the old wine is ripe and generally superior in taste. Then he describes the kinds of persons

---

[8] See Jeremy Corley, *Ben Sira's Teaching on Friendship.* BJS 316 (Providence, RI: Brown Judaic Studies, 2002).

to be avoided (9:11-13) and to be cultivated (9:14-16) as friends. Those who are to be avoided include sinners, the ungodly, and those who have the power to kill you. Those to be cultivated are the wise, intelligent, and righteous. The latter are persons who converse about "the law of the Most High" and glory in "fear of the Lord."

What should one do when a friend is accused of wrongdoing and/or is the subject of gossip? In 19:13-17 Ben Sira recommends going directly to the friend and finding out what really happened. It is possible that the friend has been falsely accused. And even if the accusation proves to be true, then a true friend can help the person work toward forgiveness and reconciliation. Having determined the truth of the matter, one should let "the law of the Most High take its course" (19:17)—a reference either to the appropriate penalties in the Torah or to the commandment to love one's neighbor as oneself (Lev 19:18).

In 22:19-26 Ben Sira gives advice about how friendships are destroyed (22:19-22, 24) and built up (22:23, 25-26). Friendships are delicate personal relationships, and friends can be easily wounded. What Ben Sira finds especially destructive are "reviling, arrogance, disclosure of secrets, or a treacherous blow—in these cases any friend will take to flight" (22:22). A true friend will seek out others in their poverty and distress, and provide shelter for them (22:23, 25). And if you are eventually betrayed by such a person, "whoever hears of it will beware of him" (22:26).

In 27:16-21 Ben Sira emphasizes the grave offense against friendship involved in revealing confidences or "secrets" about a friend. He regards such revelations as the quickest way to end a friendship. For "a wound may be bandaged, and there is reconciliation after abuse, but whoever has betrayed secrets is without hope" (27:21).

In 37:1-6 Ben Sira criticizes "fair-weather" friends and those who are friends in name only. He blames the "inclination to evil" present in every human for treacherous behavior in what proves to be only an apparent friendship. Ben Sira insists that true friends must stick together in both bad times and good times: "Do not forget a friend during the battle, and do not be unmindful of him when you distribute your spoils" (37:6).

Interfaces: Friendship is not a prominent topic for Qoheleth. The closest he comes to treating it is his "two are better than one" reflection in 4:9-12. The idea is that when two persons join together they have better results than if each goes it alone. So when two are together and one falls, the one can pick up the other. If two lie in the same bed they both will be warmer than if they sleep alone. If two are in a fight, the two together have a better chance of withstanding attack than if each acts alone. Qoheleth's approach to friendship is totally pragmatic. There is no attention to interpersonal dynamics or to the religious dimension of friendship (fear of the Lord) as there is in Sirach. Given his disposition, it is unlikely that Qoheleth had many friends.

A short and fragmentary text among the Dead Sea scrolls (4Q424) lists persons to be avoided if you want something to be done properly and wish to avoid trouble, as well as persons to be cultivated as friends on the grounds of their intellectual and moral character. The list of persons to be avoided has no surprises: liars, fools, complainers, greedy and envious persons, and so forth. Those to be sought out are the intelligent and wise (because they will accept instruction and find wisdom), the righteous or upright, persons of truth and integrity, and those who are generous to the poor.

The classic ancient treatment of friendship appears in Books 8 and 9 of Aristotle's *Nicomachean Ethics*. There is probably no better entry point to the works of Aristotle, and it ranks with Plato's *Apology* as one of the most attractive pieces of philosophy ever written. In it Aristotle provides a systematic philosophical discussion of friendship: the various kinds of friendship, the importance of reciprocity, its relation to other forms of community, the casuistry associated with it, its internal nature, and its necessity for human beings. He emphasizes reciprocal goodwill as the essence of friendship and insists that perfect friendship exists only among persons who are good and alike in virtue. While Aristotle's analysis is intellectually perceptive and realistic, there is little emotional tone and no religious dimension to it. While Aristotle's philosophical treatise operates at a much higher and more comprehensive intellectual level that Ben Sira's little instructions do, it does lack the experiential and practical elements that make Ben Sira's treatment attractive, memorable, and helpful.

In the New Testament Jesus redefines his family and extends it to encompass all those who sincerely seek to do the will of God (Mark 3:35). At the Last Supper, according to John 15:12-15, Jesus designates as the ultimate manifestation of friendship the willingness "to lay down one's life for one's friends" (15:13). Then he addresses his disciples as "friends" because they have received Jesus' revelations of himself and his heavenly father. Thus Jesus takes Ben Sira's ideal of friendship in the Lord to an even higher level.

Questions: (1) What is friendship for you, and when and why do you call someone your friend? (2) How do you make friends? (3) What do you expect from a friend? (4) What do you expect to do for a friend? (5) Why and how have your friendships ended?

Exercise 6: Sin (Key Texts in Sirach—15:11-20; 16:1-23; 17:25-32; 21:1-10; 22:26–23:6; 27:27–28:7). "He [the Lord] has not commanded anyone to be wicked, and he has not given anyone permission to sin."

Sin may be defined as a failure to love—God, our neighbor, and ourself. It involves departing from the life of virtue and turning aside from the way of wisdom. While not a major topic in secular wisdom then or now, sin is an essential part of the religious tradition of Israel (and of Christianity). The focus in Sirach and other Jewish wisdom books is what we regard as "moral" (rather than cultic) sins in which the ethical commandments of God are broken.

Ben Sira: Large parts of the middle of the book of Sirach are devoted to the topic of sin. The author seems especially interested in the origin of sin, the psychology of sin, the effects of sin, and the need for repentance. He also explores what leads people to sin, and the excuses they make for themselves.

In 15:11-20 Ben Sira chastises those who blame God for their sins, those who say: "It was the Lord's doing that I fell away . . . . It was he who led me astray" (15:11-12). He dismisses such excuses, places the responsibility for sin on the free will of the sinner, and alludes to the sin of Adam and Eve in Genesis 3: "when God created humankind in the beginning, he left them in the power of their own free choice" (15:14). What especially leads one to sin is the "inclination" or disposition of humans to try to take sovereignty away from the "God of all" and place themselves in the role that belongs to God. This evil inclination is not so much the inheritance from Adam and Eve (the classic Christian doctrine of original sin) as it is the reason why they did what they did in Genesis 3 and why humans repeat their experience. It is what makes human will free to choose life or death, and to live either in accord with God's will or to sin.

In 16:1-23 Ben Sira insists that God will surely punish sinners just as he has done throughout history, and that God is both merciful and just: "Great as his mercy, so also is his chastisement; he judges a person according to one's deeds" (16:12). Sinners who think that they can escape the attention of God, who say "I am hidden from the Lord" (16:17), are described as "devoid of understanding" and as "senseless and misguided" 16:23).

Besides analyzing sin and sinners, Ben Sira is equally interested in promoting repentance and avoidance of sin. In 17:25-32 he issues a call for repentance: "Turn back to the Lord and forsake your sins" (17:25a). He urges sinners to repent before they die and to sing God's praises in the present. He declares: "How great is the mercy of the Lord, and his forgiveness for those who return to him" (17:29). In 21:1-10 he counsels his readers to sin no more, to ask forgiveness for past sins, and to "flee from sin as from a snake" (21:2). Then after mentioning some sins and their evil effects, he warns that "the way of sinners is paved with smooth stones but at its end is the pit of Hades" (21:10). And in 22:27–23:6 Ben Sira provides a question-

and-answer segment on who can prevent him from sinning with his words and his thoughts. The answers take the form of prayers of petition directed to the "Lord, Father, and Master [God] of my life" for help in overcoming temptations to sin.

In 27:30–28:7 Ben Sira affirms a principle also emphasized by Jesus in the Lord's Prayer (see Matt 6:12; Luke 11:4). If we expect God to forgive our sins, then we must be ready to forgive others for their sins against us. In 28:2 Ben Sira states: "Forgive your neighbor for the wrong he has done, and then your sins will be pardoned when you pray."

Interfaces: When these and related passages are put together, the book of Sirach emerges as the most extensive and comprehensive treatment of sin among the biblical wisdom books. It provides a solid foundation for understanding how the Bible approaches the topic. However, other wisdom books also make important contributions regarding sin. The instructions in the first nine chapters of Proverbs to pursue wisdom (and righteousness) and to avoid folly (and sin) illustrate the emphasis also found in Sirach on free will and the power to choose the way on which one is to walk in life. The book of Job is an extensive exploration of the relation between sin and suffering. Job's friends are convinced that because Job is suffering he must have sinned. But Job consistently and correctly protests that he has not sinned, and so he searches for some other rational explanation or cause for his suffering. According to Wisdom 13–14 (and Rom 1:18-32), the failure to worship the one true God led humans (before and apart from Christ) ever deeper into the downward spiral of sin.

With regard to the origin of sin, the tradition found in *1 Enoch* 6–16 and Revelation 12 (see Gen 6:1-4) blames the presence of sin in the world on the rebellion and fall of certain dissident angels within the heavenly court. In Romans 5, Paul goes back to the account of the "original sin" of Adam and Eve in Genesis 3 and traces the spread of sin and death to the pattern set by the ancestors of all humans—a pattern that all humans before and apart from Christ repeat (see Rom 7:7-25).

Questions: (1) How do you understand and define sin? (2) What kinds of actions or attitudes do you regard as sinful? (3) Why do you (and other people) sin? (4) What excuses do you (and other people) give when caught in sin? (5) What negative effects does sin have?

Exercise 7: Why Evil? (Key Texts in Sirach—33:7-15; 39:12-35). "Look at all the works of the Most High; they come in pairs, one the opposite of the other" (33:15).

The "problem" of evil came to the fore especially with Israel's exile in Babylon. Most of Israel's prophets blamed the sufferings of their people on their own sins and especially on the sins of their kings and leaders. At the same time, the prophet now called "Second Isaiah" (the one responsible for Isaiah 40–55) made far-reaching claims about the God of Israel as the only real God. One of those claims concerns this God's omnipotence, even over evil: "I form light and create darkness, I make weal and create woe; I the LORD do all these things" (45:7). While the prophet's emphasis is clearly on God's unlimited sovereignty over all creation, the text also could suggest that this same God was therefore responsible for "darkness" and "woe."

Ben Sira: In confronting the problem of evil Ben Sira offers no definition of evil, nor does he refer to anything like a Satan figure. Rather, he takes "evil" as a fact of existence that he had to explain in view of his conviction that the God of Israel is the "Lord of all," and indeed the only God.

In 33:7-15 Ben Sira moves toward what can be called a "modified dualism," that is, a stance that affirms the ultimate sovereignty of God while acknowledging the presence of evil, death, and sin in the world: "Good is the opposite of evil, and life is the opposite of death; so the sinner is the opposite of the godly" (33:14). He urges his readers to look at all the works of God and to recognize that "they come in pairs, one the opposite of the other" (33:15). In leading up to this conclusion Ben Sira first reflects on the differences among the days of the year (33:7-9). Some days are holydays and so are exalted, and other days are ordinary. Yet God makes them all, and causes the same sun to shine on them all. In 33:10-13 Ben Sira offers the more serious example of differences among human beings. All humans come from the same "ground," and yet some are "blessed and exalted" while others are "cursed and brought low." The reason is to be traced to God, who is compared to a potter who molds clay to make "whatever he decides." This example is intended to explain why there are different kinds of people when there is only one God who creates all things. While affirming the sovereignty of the one God, Ben Sira takes a step toward admitting a kind of dualism in the world and in human existence by his doctrine of the "pairs": "Look at all the works of the Most High; they come in pairs, one the opposite of the other" (33:15).

In his hymn of praise to God (39:12-35) Ben Sira proclaims that "all the works of the Lord are very good" (39:16) and that "everything has been created for its own purpose" (39:21). These basic affirmations of Jewish theology lead Ben Sira to offer still other explanations of the presence of evil in the world. In 39:25 he contends that "from the beginning good things were created for the good, but for sinners good things and bad." After listing the basic necessities of life (water, fire, iron, salt, wheat flour, milk, honey, wine, oil, and clothing), he contends that all these are good for good persons, "but for sinners they turn into evils" (39:27). The idea seems to be that good persons use these basic necessities properly, while the wicked use them in perverse ways and suffer their evil consequences.

In 39:28-31 Ben Sira puts forward the notion that some things created by God (and so good in themselves) can serve to mete out justice to the wicked. The examples he gives concern winds, fire, hail, famine, pestilence, wild animals, scorpions and vipers, and the sword. Though objectively good, they can be used by God to punish the ungodly with destruction. In other words, they can serve as divine instruments for upholding the law of retribution and for affirming the connection between sin and suffering.

By way of conclusion in 39:32-35, Ben Sira reaffirms that "all the works of the Lord are good" (39:33; see 39:16), and adds that "everything proves good in its appointed time" (39:34). One gets the impression from the "hymn" that Ben Sira has taken on a difficult topic and is casting about in search of various arguments: God's constitution of creation in pairs, the bad use to which evil people put God's creations, God's use of his creations to punish the wicked, and the matter of timing. No one of these considerations is totally convincing on its own

Interfaces: Qoheleth was, of course, fully aware of the presence of evil in the world, but he gave up on trying to explain it and dismissed such attempts as another case of "vanity" (emptiness, nonsense, futility). He insists that there is no necessary connection between behavior and its consequences in this life. He observes that "there are righteous people who perish in their righteousness, and there are wicked people who prolong their life in their evil doing" (7:15). And while celebrating that there is "a time to be born and a time to die" and so forth (3:2-8), he also notes that it is very difficult (if not impossible) for humans to "find out what God has done from beginning to end" (3:11). In other words, there may well be a time for all these things, but we do not know when that time is.

At the opposite end of the spectrum from Qoheleth's skepticism lies the instruction found in the Qumran *Rule of the Community,* columns 3 and 4. Whereas Ben Sira timidly asserted the existence of "pairs" in creation, the Qumran text elaborates the doctrine of the pairs into an almost metaphysical explanation of all reality—past, present, and future. Whereas Ben Sira proposed a "modified dualism" that affirmed God's sovereignty while allowing for different kinds of entities and persons (good and evil, life and death, sinner and godly), the Qumran text adds a future or apocalyptic dimension in which the cosmic struggle between the pairs is to be ended definitively by divine intervention.

The Qumran instruction is presented as what the spiritual guide or religious superior of the community is to hand on to new members as the theological foundation on which they are to base their lives. The instruction begins by asserting the absolute sovereignty of God: "From the God of knowledge comes all that is and shall be . . . . The laws of all things are in his hand." Having given to humans sovereignty over the world in the present ("to govern the world"), God has also created for them "two spirits in which to walk until the time of His visitation." These two spirits are personified as the "Prince of Light" (something like Michael the archangel) and the "Angel of Darkness" (something like a Satan figure). Until the time of God's final visitation humans are to live and act under the dominion of one of these two "leaders." So the children of light do the (good) deeds of light under the Prince of Light, while the children of darkness do the (evil) deeds of darkness under the Angel of Darkness. This cosmic struggle goes on until the time appointed by God for putting an end to falsehood (including the Angel of Darkness, the children of darkness, and all their evil deeds).

The dualism sketched in the Qumran *Rule of the Community* goes far beyond what Ben Sira suggests in its doctrine of the "two powers," in its comprehensive vision of human and cosmic existence, and in explaining the presence of evil in a way that protects the divine omnipotence and envisions an end to all evil in the (near) future.

This kind of modified apocalyptic dualism seems to have been the presupposition of several New Testament writings and especially of Paul's letter to the Romans (see chapters 1–8 for many examples). Of course, Paul affirms the absolute sovereignty of the God of Israel. He views humans before and apart from Christ as being led astray by the combined forces of three "powers"—Sin, Death, and the Law. In Paul's adaptation of the schema Christ and/or the Holy Spirit is the positive or good power, and Paul looks forward to the coming of the fullness of God's kingdom as the decisive divine intervention. The distinctive feature in the early Christian version is the claim that the definitive intervention has already begun in and through Jesus' life, death, and resurrection.

Questions: (1) What persons, things, events, etc. constitute "evil" for you? (2) How do you define "evil"? (3) Do you see any empirical basis for the doctrine of the "pairs"? (4) Which approach (if any) do you find most convincing: Ben Sira, Qoheleth, the Qumran *Rule of the Community,* or Paul? Why? (5) How do you explain the presence of evil in the world?

Exercise 8: Mourning, Death, and Afterlife (Key Texts in Sirach— 22:11-22; 38:16-23; 41:1-13). "The days of a good life are numbered, but a good name lasts forever" (41:13).

Every serious philosophical and religious thinker must give attention to the issues surrounding death and life after death. Ben Sira's positions, while in line with much of the Hebrew Bible and not as skeptical as Qoheleth's, may seem inadequate to those who embrace classical Judaism and Christianity. However, as on most topics, Ben Sira expresses himself with clarity and offers a challenge to those who want to go beyond him regarding afterlife expectations.

Ben Sira: In 22:11-12 Ben Sira contrasts weeping for the dead and weeping for a fool. Whereas the dead person is "at rest," and mourning for the dead lasts only seven days, weeping for foolish or ungodly persons lasts "all the days of their lives."

In 38:16-23 Ben Sira provides instructions about the dangers of excessive mourning for the dead. He begins in 38:16-17 by encouraging the sage to participate in laying out the corpse, attending to the burial rites, and performing the customary weeping and wailing. But these activities should last "for one day or two" (rather than seven days!), mainly to avoid scandal or gossip. Then one should feel free to move on with one's life. This advice may sound callous and/or calculating. The emotional or psychological reason (38:18-20) is that excessive grief and mourning can result in sickness and even death. The more philosophical reason (38:21-23) is that since "there is no coming back" from death and "the dead are at rest," there is nothing to be gained by excessive grief and mourning. In fact, the death of a loved one should be the occasion for reflecting on one's own death: "Remember his fate, for yours is like it; yesterday it was his, and today it is yours" (38:22). Excessive grief cannot help one whose "spirit has departed."

A more explicit reflection on death and life after death appears in 41:1-13. In 41:1-4 Ben Sira insists that death is inevitable and final. Death may be bitter for someone who is prosperous and healthy, but welcome for one who is poor, old, weak, and despondent. Nevertheless, death remains "the Lord's decree for all flesh" (41:4). Whatever afterlife Ben Sira may allow for one whose "spirit has departed" is at most a shadowy existence in Sheol or Hades, the traditional gloomy abode of the dead where no questions are asked or answered.

One traditional Jewish (and almost universal) approach to life after death takes the form of achieving immortality through one's children. In many cultures one is thought to live on through one's descendants, and in turn the ancestors are honored in a way that can even look like worship. Ben Sira was surely familiar with this kind of thinking. While not rejecting it entirely, he does challenge it. His point is that the value of such a form of immortality depends too much on the moral quality of one's children. According to 41:5-7 sinners tend to produce "abominable children," and children suffer disgrace from ungodly parents. For those "who have forsaken the law of the Most High God" (41:8), immortality through children is worse than oblivion or total annihilation. On the contrary, a "virtuous name will never be blotted out" (41:11). Such a name is said to last longer than a thousand hoards of gold. Indeed, "a good name lasts forever" (41:13).

Ben Sira teaches that death is inevitable for humans, that some mourning for the dead is appropriate but must not be excessive, and that death is final. Rather than seeking immortality through one's children, the best route to "immortality" is to lead a good and virtuous life (which means observing the law of the Most High God) and so to deserve a virtuous and good "name" (reputation, memory) that will last forever.

Interfaces: Qoheleth's view of death and life after death, while even gloomier, is not far from that of Ben Sira. He places humans in the same category as animals: "All go to one place; all are from the dust, and all turn to dust again" (3:20). Indeed, a living animal has an advantage, since "a living dog is better than a dead lion" (9:4). According to Qoheleth, "the dead know nothing; they have no reward, and even the memory of them is lost" (9:5). Qoheleth's marvelous picture of the physical decay that accompanies old age concludes that "dust returns to the earth as it was, and the breath returns to God who gave it" (12:7).

Ben Sira's conservative and even minimalist views on life after death provoked subtle (and not so subtle) responses even from his own translators. In the Greek translation the grandson inserted a reference to "fire and worms" as punishments for the ungodly (7:17b; see Mark 9:48) and a claim that "we also shall surely live" (48:11b). The more expansive Greek version mentions "an everlasting gift with joy" for those who fear the Lord (2:9c) and "a scrutiny for all . . . at the end" (16:22c). It also promises to those who do what is pleasing to God that they will "enjoy the fruit of the tree of immortality" (19:19b). The Syriac and Old Latin versions contain even more explicit references to rewards and punishments after death and to eternal life and sharing in the lot of the holy ones (angels).

Between the composition of Ben Sira's book in Hebrew (around 180 B.C.E.) and his grandson's translation of it into Greek (around 117 B.C.E.), there were important developments among Jews in Israel and in the Diaspora pertaining to beliefs about life after death. Ben Sira with his vision of Sheol as the shadowy abode of the dead was in line with most of the Hebrew Bible. Even the wonderful vision of "resurrection" in the Valley of Dry Bones in Ezek 37:1-14 is a grand metaphor for the rebirth of Israel as a nation after the exile of its leaders to Babylon in the sixth century B.C.E. But the book of Daniel, written around 165 B.C.E., looks forward to a literal resurrection of the dead: "Many of those who sleep in the dust of the earth shall awake, some to everlasting life, and some to shame and everlasting contempt" (12:2). Those who have proved themselves to be wise and righteous will shine "like the stars forever and ever" (12:3).

Belief in immortality after death was taken up in the first-century book of Wisdom ("the souls of the righteous are in the hand of God," 3:1) and in 2 Maccabees (especially in 7:1-42 and 12:43-45). In New Testament times the Sadducees seem to have maintained the more traditional Jewish position held by Ben Sira (see Acts 23:8), while the Pharisees became the great proponents of resurrection and of rewards and punishments after death. According to Mark 12:18-27, Jesus agreed with the Pharisees on this matter over against the Sadducees.

Questions: (1) Can mourning for the dead really be excessive? (2) Does Ben Sira's attitude seem callous? (3) Do you believe in life after death? If so, what form do you think it will take? (4) Do you find a connection between having children and the desire for immortality? (5) Does a good name really last forever?

Exercise 9: God's Glory Made Manifest in Creation (Key Texts in Sirach—42:15–43:33). "The work of the Lord is full of his glory" (42:16b).

One of the most important goals of the Spiritual Exercises of Ignatius of Loyola is to help the exercitant to "find God in all things." Ben Sira had the same idea many centuries before. His vision of creation encourages a proper balance between admiring and loving "nature" on the one hand and recognizing and appreciating the "Lord of all" who created it and stands behind it. For Ben Sira, God's creation is a kind of "sacrament," that is, an outward sign that points to the presence and glory of God. In our time when there is great concern about environmental issues, the "sacramental" view of nature promoted by Ben Sira may aid us in looking upon nature not simply as a resource to be exploited but rather as a manifestation of God's glory.

Ben Sira: The author draws his wisdom book to a close not with more wise maxims or instructions, but rather with hymnic celebrations of the glory of God made manifest first in creation (42:15–43:33) and then in the heroes of Israel's history (44:1–50:24). In both cases the proper response to these manifestations of God's glory is praise (see 43:27-33 and 50:22-24).

The celebration of God's glory made manifest in creation consists of three main parts: the power of God in creation (42:15-25), the marvels of God in the heavens and on earth (43:1-26), and the call to praise God the Creator and Lord of all (43:27-33). For Ben Sira the world around us is both an occasion for learning about God's glory and a motive for giving praise to God. In Ben Sira's view there is a kind of "sacramental" dimension to God's creation insofar as it serves as a sign pointing to the glory of God.

The God of Ben Sira is absolutely sovereign, awesome and mighty, and beyond the capacity of humans to comprehend and appreciate fully. Not only is this God the all-wise creator, but he has even poured his wisdom into all creation. And yet he remains the caring and merciful one in his dealings with his people.

The first section (42:15-25) stresses the omnipotence and omniscience of God, with several comments about the wise order God has imposed on creation: "by the word of the Lord his works are made" (42:15). This reflection is punctuated by references to the glory of God manifest in creation: "the work of the Lord is full of his glory" (42:16b); "so that the universe may stand firm in his glory" (42:17); and "Who could ever tire of seeing his glory?" (42:25).

The part devoted to the marvels of creation in the heavens (43:1-12) describes the "higher realms" as "glorious to behold" (43:1), and goes into some detail about how God's glory can be glimpsed in the sun, the moon, the stars, and the rainbow. In 43:9 Ben Sira declares that "the glory of the stars is the beauty of heaven," and in 43:12 he notes how the "glorious arc" of the rainbow encircles the sky. The part concerning the marvels of creation on earth (43:13-26) shows how various forces of nature—snow, lightning, clouds, hail, thunder, earthquakes, wind, and so on—provide glimpses of God's power and glory. These forces of nature function "by his plan" (43:23), and the whole passage is summarized by the statement: "by his word all things hold together" (43:26).

The call to praise in 43:27-33 comes as the proper response to all these manifestations of God's glory. However, Ben Sira is fully aware of the inadequacy of human praise when God is its object. He says: "let the final word be: 'He is the all' . . . he is greater than all his works"(43:27-28). The Lord is awesome and great, and his power is indeed marvelous. And so however much humans try to "glorify" him, they always fall short. The marvels of creation teach us how little we know about God—not by way of inducing skepticism but rather by forcing us to recognize that we "have seen but few of his works" (43:32). The celebration ends with a statement that summarizes the passage and indeed the whole book of Sirach: "For the Lord has made all things, and to the godly he has given wisdom" (43:33). For some other important passages in Sirach about God and creation see 16:24–17:24; 18:1-14; 33:7-15; and 39:12-35.

Interfaces: Much in Ben Sira's celebration of God's glory in creation (42:15–43:33) sounds like material in the Lord's speech from the whirlwind in Job 38:1–39:30. Both texts emphasize the divine sovereignty over all creation and the human inability to grasp fully God's plan for his creation. But the tone is quite different. Whereas Ben Sira wants us to reflect positively on how God's glory is revealed in the heavens and on earth and to summon us to praise God, the author of Job appears more interested in putting Job "in his place" and in cutting off his questions and complaints.

While Proverbs does not give much space to creation, its famous description of Wisdom as a female personal figure in 8:22-36 makes a link between Wisdom and God's act of creation ("the Lord created me at the beginning of his work," 8:22), and suggests that those who listen to Wisdom and accept her instruction will find life and favor from the Lord (8:35). The book of Wisdom presents the figure of Wisdom as a kind of "world soul" animating the cosmos ("the spirit of the Lord has filled the world and . . . holds all things together,"1:7), and describes Wisdom as "a spirit that is intelligent, holy, unique, manifold, subtle, mobile, clear, unpolluted . . ." (7:22). The consequence of this vision of creation is that all creation is shot through with the wisdom and the glory of God, and so the "sacramental" dimension hinted at by Ben Sira is heightened greatly.

The New Testament takes this "sacramental" vision of creation in a christological direction. The letter to the Hebrews 1:3 describes the risen Christ in terms used in Wisdom 7 ("the reflection of God's glory and the exact imprint of God's very being") and asserts that "he sustains all things by his powerful word." The Wisdom hymn preserved in Col 1:15-20 also links the risen Christ with creation: "all things have been created through him and for him. He himself is before all things, and in him all things hold together" (1:16-17). The use of wisdom terminology in turn gives an important cosmic dimension to christology and has the effect of making the world around us into a sign of the glory of God made manifest in the resurrection of Jesus.

Questions: (1) Where do you find God? (2) Do you ever find God in the world around you? (3) Is there is any one place that is especially conducive to your finding God? Why? (4) Have you ever considered nature to be a sacrament? (5) Do you praise God for the beauty of nature?

Exercise 10: God's Glory Made Manifest in Israel's History (Key Texts in Sirach—chs. 44–50). "Let us now sing the praises of glorious men, our ancestors in their generations. The Lord apportioned to them great glory, his majesty from the beginning" (44:1-2).

Both Jews and Christians believe that God has worked in and through history and the great figures who made that history. If we can regard nature as a sacrament of God's glory, it is also possible to find the hand of God at work in the figures of biblical history. In that sense Ben Sira presents Israel's history as a "sacrament."

Ben Sira: One of the most famous parts of Ben Sira's book is his catalogue of heroes in chapters 44–50. After a prologue (44:1-15), it moves from Enoch in Genesis 5 down to Ben Sira's own time, climaxing with a wonderful portrait of the Jewish high priest, Simon son of Onias, presiding at a rite of sacrifice in the Jerusalem Temple.

The catalogue begins with the theme of glory: "the praises of glorious men" (44:1). Its theme is stated in the second verse: "The Lord apportioned to them great glory" (44:2). When Ben Sira finally comes to introduce Simon the high priest and to describe him presiding at the Temple sacrifice, he exclaims in 50:5: "How glorious he was!" In Ben Sira's catalogue of biblical heroes, the great figures he selects for discussion are generally manifestations of the glory of God. In other words, God is the primary actor in salvation history, and Israel's "heroes" are reflections of God's glory.

Everything in Ben Sira's catalogue leads up to his presentation of Simon the high priest, and so his catalogue is a highly selective retelling of the biblical narrative. It includes no women! It gives particular emphasis to figures associated in the Bible with the theme of the covenant and the cultic complex of the Israelite priesthood, temple worship, and sacrifice. But the motif that ties everything together is "glory." This is the lens through which Ben Sira views God's actions with and for Israel in salvation history.

In his prologue Ben Sira lists the various kinds of persons counted among Israel's heroes, and promises that "their glory will never be blotted out" (44:13). In describing Moses in 44:23–45:5, he claims in 45:2 that God made Moses "equal in glory to the holy ones" (angels), and revealed to him "his glory" in giving the commandments on Mount Sinai (45:3). In his expansive description of Aaron the priest (foreshadowing Simon the priest) Ben Sira notes that God "added glory to Aaron and gave him a heritage" (45:20). In introducing the zealous priest Phinehas, Ben Sira notes that he "ranks third in glory" (45:23) to Moses and Aaron, and concludes with a blessing acknowledging that God has crowned his people with glory and prays that "their glory may endure through all generations" (45:26).

In describing the military successes of Joshua in 46:1-10, Ben Sira proclaims: "How glorious he was when he lifted his hands and brandished his sword against the cities!" (46:2). When treating the deeds of King David in 47:2-11, Ben Sira observes that the people "glorified him" for his conquests and that a "glorious diadem was given to him" (47:6), and that after his victories David gave thanks to God by "proclaiming his glory" (47:8) and that God in turn forgave David's sins and gave him "a covenant of kingship and a glorious throne in Israel" (47:11).

While Solomon (47:12-22) is praised for his wisdom and splendor, he is criticized for giving in to his sexual passions and so staining his honor and defiling his family line, thus besmirching the glory of God. On the contrary, the prophet Elijah (48:1-11) is presented as a genuine manifestation of God's glory: "How glorious you were, Elijah, in your wondrous deeds! Whose glory is equal to yours?" (48:4).

In admitting that most of Judah's kings were sinners (49:4), Ben Sira accuses them of giving "their glory to a foreign nation" (49:6), thus alluding to the capture of Jerusalem and its temple by the Babylonians in 587 B.C.E. However, he notes that during the exile the prophet Ezekiel saw "the vision of glory" (49:8), and that the leaders of those Jews who returned from the exile such as Zerubbabel and Joshua the priest "raised a temple holy to the Lord, destined for everlasting glory" (49:12).

According to Ben Sira a climactic point in Israel's history comes with the high priest of his own day, Simon son of Onias. He was high priest from 219 to 196 B.C.E. and carried out many public works projects for the fortification and beautification of the Jerusalem Temple (50:1-4). He may even have been a mentor or patron of Ben Sira. As we have seen, Ben Sira was an enthusiastic supporter of the Jerusalem Temple and its rituals. In a real sense the whole catalogue of biblical heroes in Sirach 44–50 was very likely intended as a tribute to the memory of (the then recently deceased?) Simon the high priest.[9]

When Ben Sira describes Simon presiding at the sacrifice for the Day of Atonement (or perhaps simply the Tamid, or daily offering), he begins by acclaiming: "How glorious he was!" (50:5). In 50:6-10 he compares Simon's appearance to a whole set of glorious sights: the morning star, the full moon, the sun shining, the rainbow, roses, lilies, a green shoot on Lebanon, fire and incense, a vessel of hammered gold, an olive tree laden with fruit, and a cypress towering in the clouds. From the description in 50:12-21 one can discern some of the elements of the liturgy at which Simon presided: receiving the sacrifice, pouring out the drink offering or libation, the blowing of trumpets and the people's prostration, singing and praying, and the high priest's final blessing and the people's prostration. This is altogether a glorious scene.

Ben Sira, the scribe-sage and student of Israel's Scriptures, found no contradiction with adherence to the Jewish Temple rituals and priesthood. In fact, it has been suggested that his own school was somehow connected with the Jerusalem Temple. He chose to place Simon the high priest and his ritual sacrifice at the Temple as the figure to which all of biblical history and its heroes were pointing. Indeed, his enthusiasm for the Temple and its priesthood influenced his entire presentation of biblical history, and so he came to view the Temple ritual as a climactic manifestation of the glory of God. As is the case throughout his handbook, Ben Sira is a master at combining and integrating various strands of tradition and taking the best of each at its most positive value.

[9] See Otto Mulder, *Simon the High Priest in Sirach 50*. JSJSup 78 (Leiden: Brill, 2003).

Interfaces: In contrast to Ben Sira, most of the wisdom books of the ancient Near East and the Bible show little or no explicit interest in history *per se.* The great exception is the author of the book of Wisdom. In the second half of his book he examines the role of personified Wisdom in early biblical history. The point is that through Wisdom God was at work in the events that led up to and included Israel's liberation from slavery in Egypt.

In Wisdom 10 the author covers the period from Adam to Moses. He avoids giving proper names in favor of vague descriptions that nonetheless no reader with basic biblical knowledge could miss. For example, the "first-formed father of the world" is clearly Adam. The "anonymity" of the heroes seems to have been a rhetorical device aimed at engaging the reader in a kind of Bible quiz.

What did Wisdom do in early history? First she made it possible for Adam, even though he had sinned, to "rule all things" (10:1). When Cain killed Abel "he departed from her" (Wisdom), and so he perished (10:2-3). It was Wisdom who saved the earth from the great flood in Noah's time (10:4) and preserved Abraham blameless in the Tower of Babel episode and kept him strong when he was called upon to sacrifice Isaac (10:5). It was Wisdom who rescued Lot from the destruction of the five cities (10:6-8), Jacob from his enemies (10:9-12), and Joseph from his false accusers (10:13-14).

But Wisdom's greatest feats took place on behalf of Israel during the exodus from Egypt: "A holy people and blameless race wisdom delivered from a nation of oppressors" (10:15; see 18:15). It was Wisdom who entered into Moses, guided Israel out of Egypt, led them to praise God, and "prospered their works by the hand of a holy prophet" (11:1). This catalogue of Wisdom's activities in and through great figures in Israel's early history sets the stage for the author's theological reflections on the Exodus in chapters 11 through 19.

Another catalogue of biblical heroes appears in 1 Macc 2:51-60 as part of the farewell discourse by the priest Mattathias at the beginning of the Maccabean revolt. First Maccabees (not a wisdom book) describes events in the land of Israel in the second century B.C.E., shortly after Ben Sira wrote his book. Mattathias was a priest in Israel, and his sons—especially Judas, Jonathan, and Simon—were the leaders of a successful revolt that eventually extricated Judea from the political control of the Seleucids and led to independence, at least until Roman control became ever more pervasive in the first century. The examples Mattathias gives involve biblical figures who remained faithful in times of testing. He promises that if his sons remember these deeds, they too "will receive great honor and an everlasting name" (2:51). In making his case Mattathias appeals to the deeds of the ancestors—Abraham, Joseph, Phinehas, Samuel, Elijah, and Daniel and his companions. The point of this catalogue becomes clear in 1 Macc 2:61: "And so observe, from generation to generation, that none of those who put their trust in him [God] will lack strength." In light of these examples of courage in the face of danger, Mattathias' advice to his sons is this: "be courageous and grow strong in the law, for by it you will gain honor" (2:64).

Still another catalogue of biblical heroes appears in Hebrews 11 (not a wisdom book but a sermon in written form). What distinguishes the list in Hebrews 11 is the repetition of the refrain "by faith." For the author of Hebrews, faith involves the knowledge of unseen realities, a generous response to God's call, a hopeful trust in God's promises, and faithful endurance in the face of suffering and death. After an introduction in Heb 11:1-3, this catalogue treats primeval figures such as Abel, Enoch, and Noah (11:4-7); Abraham and Sarah, and other patriarchs (11:8-22); Moses, the Israelites, and Rahab (11:23-31); and other heroes mentioned in passing (11:32-38). The conclusion (11:39-40) underscores the author's basic point. If these heroes of old could remain faithful in trying circumstances, how much more should those who live in the time of Jesus Christ be faithful. Hebrews 11 is a Christian reading of Israel's past, and its inclusion of women (unlike Ben Sira) seems to be part of its emphasis on marginal figures ("strangers and exiles") as real heroes of faith.

Questions: (1) Can history serve as a sacrament of God's glory? Why or why not? (2) Which of the biblical figures in these lists do you find most attractive? Why? (3) If you were to make a list of biblical and post-biblical heroes of faith, who would you include? (4) What principles would guide you in drawing up your list? (5) Does anyone you know personally serve as a hero of faith for you?

Conclusion

These "spiritual exercises" are intended to illustrate a method for reading Ben Sira's book and better appreciating Ben Sira's person and teaching. This approach recognizes that he treats topics in different places in his book and from different angles. When we draw some of these passages together we can better understand his views on important matters. We see that Ben Sira was willing to take on such major topics as the nature of wisdom, fear of the Lord, friendship, the "denial" psychology of sinners, the presence of evil in the world, dealing with death, and God's activity in creation and Israel's history.

These "spiritual exercises" also show that Ben Sira should be regarded as a major voice within Second Temple Judaism. He had opinions on practically everything and stated them forcefully. Though not the most profound among his literary peers, Ben Sira generally represents a balanced perspective on most issues (except women!). Even where his deficiencies are manifest, as in his struggling with the problem of evil, we can see that he is usually moving in the right directions. When we read his key texts together, we ourselves are challenged to think them through for ourselves and answer the questions he raises. When we set his views beside those of other Jewish, Greek, and Christian writers, we find that there were diverse views in antiquity even among authors whose books made it into the Bible. Studying Ben Sira and his book under the rubric of "spiritual exercises" is a good way of doing biblical theology.

Ben Sira's varied, artistic, and interesting ways of conveying his message reveal him to have been a careful and imaginative teacher. His wisdom teachings provide a window into the social structures and values of Second Temple Judaism. His double emphasis on the search for divine wisdom and on fear of the Lord gives spiritual depth to all his teachings. Perhaps his greatest achievement lay in his ability to integrate the many different strands of biblical piety: wisdom, Torah, worship, prophecy, creation, and history. His conviction that creation and Israel's history show forth the glory of God offers a wonderful way of looking at the world and our place within it. But the most important lesson we can learn from Jesus Ben Sira today is that the quest for wisdom never ends. Ben Sira himself makes this point in a memorable way: "When human beings have finished, they are just beginning; and when they stop, they are still perplexed" (18:7).

FOR REFERENCE
AND FURTHER STUDY

Beentjes, Pancratius C. *The Book of Ben Sira in Hebrew.* VTSup 68. Leiden: Brill, 1997.

_____, ed. *The Book of Ben Sira in Modern Research.* BZAW 255. Berlin and New York: de Gruyter, 1997.

Camp, Claudia. *Wisdom and the Feminine in the Book of Proverbs.* Sheffield: Almond, 1985.

Clifford, Richard J. *Proverbs.* Louisville: Westminster John Knox, 1999.

_____. *The Wisdom Literature.* Nashville: Abingdon, 1998.

Coggins, Richard J. *Sirach.* Guides to Apocrypha and Pseudepigrapha. Sheffield: Sheffield Academic Press, 1998.

Collins, John J. *Jewish Wisdom in the Hellenistic Age.* Louisville: Westminster John Knox, 1997.

Corley, Jeremy. *Ben Sira's Teaching on Friendship.* BJS 316. Providence, RI: Brown Judaic Studies, 2002.

Crenshaw, James L. "The Book of Sirach." In *The New Interpreter's Bible.* Nashville: Abingdon, 1997, 5:601–867.

_____. *Old Testament Wisdom: An Introduction.* Louisville: Westminster John Knox, 1998.

deSilva, David A. "The Wisdom of Ben Sira: Honor, Shame, and the Maintenance of the Values of a Minority Culture," *CBQ* 58 (1996) 433–55.

Deutsch, Celia M. *Lady Wisdom, Jesus, and the Sages. Metaphor and Social Context in Matthew's Gospel.* Harrisburg, PA: Trinity Press International, 1997.

Egger-Wenzel, Renate, ed. *Ben Sira's God.* BZAW 321. Berlin: de Gruyter, 2001.

Fox, Michael V. *Proverbs 1–9.* AB 19A. New York: Doubleday, 2000.

Gutiérrez, Gustavo. *On Job: God-Talk and the Suffering of the Innocent.* Maryknoll, NY: Orbis, 1987.

Habel, Norman. *The Book of Job.* Philadelphia: Westminster, 1985.

Hadot, Pierre. *Philosophy as a Way of Life: Spiritual Exercises from Socrates to Foucault.* Oxford: Blackwell, 1995.

_____. *What Is Ancient Philosophy?* Cambridge: Harvard University Press, 2002.

Harrington, Daniel J. "Ben Sira as a Spiritual Master," *Journal of Spiritual Formation* 15 (1994) 147–57.

_____. *The Gospel of Matthew.* SP 1. Collegeville: Liturgical Press, 1991.

_____. *Invitation to the Apocrypha.* Grand Rapids: Eerdmans, 1999.

_____. *Wisdom Texts from Qumran.* London: Routledge, 1996.

Hartin, Patrick J. *James*. SP 14. Collegeville: Liturgical Press, 2003.

_____. *James of Jerusalem*. Interfaces. Collegeville: Liturgical Press, 2004.

Harvey, J. D. "Toward a Degree of Order in Ben Sira's Book," *ZAW* 105 (1993) 52–62.

Heaton, Eric W. *The School Tradition of the Old Testament*. New York: Oxford University Press, 1994.

Hengel, Martin. *Judaism and Hellenism*. Philadelphia: Fortress, 1974.

Kolarcik, Michael. "Book of Wisdom." In *The New Interpreter's Bible*. Nashville: Abingdon, 1997, 5:435–600.

Lee, Thomas R. *Studies in the Form of Sirach 44–50*. SBLDS 75. Atlanta: Scholars, 1986.

Leeuwen, Raymond van. "Proverbs." In *The New Interpreter's Bible*. Nashville: Abingdon, 1997, 5:17–264.

Liesen, Jan. *Full of Praise: An Exegetical Study of Sir 39,12-35*. JSJSup 64. Leiden: Brill, 1999.

Mack, Burton L. *Wisdom and the Hebrew Epic: Ben Sira's Hymn in Praise of the Fathers*. Chicago and London: University of Chicago Press, 1985.

Malina, Bruce J. *The New Testament World: Insights from Cultural Anthropology*. 3rd, rev. ed. Louisville: Westminster John Knox, 2001.

Mulder, Otto. *Simon the High Priest in Sirach 50*. JSJSup 78. Leiden: Brill 2003.

Murphy, Roland E. *Ecclesiastes*. WBC 23. Dallas: Word Books, 1992.

_____. *Proverbs*. WBC 18A. Waco: Word Books, 1998.

_____. *The Tree of Life: An Exploration of Biblical Wisdom Literature*. Grand Rapids: Eerdmans, 1990 (rev. ed. 2002).

Newsom, Carol. "Job." In *The New Interpreter's Bible*. Nashville: Abingdon, 1997, 4:317–637.

Okoye, John I. *Speech in Ben Sira with Special Reference to 5,9–6,1*. Frankfurt: Peter Lang, 1995.

Pilch, John J., and Bruce J. Malina, eds. *Handbook of Biblical Social Values*. Peabody, MA: Hendrickson, 1998.

Rad, Gerhard von. *Wisdom in Israel*. Nashville: Abingdon, 1972.

Roth, Wolgang. "Sirach: The First Graded Curriculum," *TBT* 29 (1991) 298–302.

Sanders, Jack T. *Ben Sira and Demotic Wisdom*. SBLMS 28. Chico: Scholars, 1983.

Seow, Choon-Leong. *Ecclesiastes*. AB 18C. New York: Doubleday, 1997.

Skehan, Patrick W., and Alexander A. Di Lella. *The Wisdom of Ben Sira*. AB 39. New York: Doubleday, 1987.

Towner, W. Sibley. "Ecclesiastes." In *The New Interpreter's Bible*. Nashville: Abingdon, 1997, 5:265–360.

Trenchard, Warren C. *Ben Sira's View of Women: A Literary Analysis*. BJS 38. Chico: Scholars, 1982.

Westermann, Claus. *Roots of Wisdom: The Oldest Proverbs of Israel and Other Peoples*. Louisville: Westminster, 1994.

Williams, D. S. "The Date of Ecclesiasticus," *VT* 44 (1994) 563–66.

Winston, David. *The Wisdom of Solomon*. AB 43. Garden City, NY: Doubleday, 1979.

Witherington, Ben C. *Jesus the Sage: The Pilgrimage of Wisdom*. Minneapolis: Fortress, 1994.

Wright, Ben G. *No Small Difference: Sirach's Relationship to its Hebrew Parent Text*. Society of Biblical Literature Septuagint and Cognate Studies 26. Atlanta: Scholars, 1989.

Yadin, Yigael. *The Ben Sira Scroll from Masada*. Jerusalem: Israel Exploration Society, 1965.

Ziegler, Joseph, ed. *Sapientia Iesu Filii Sirach*. Septuaginta 12/2. Göttingen: Vandenhoeck & Ruprecht, 1965.

INDEX OF PRINCIPAL ANCIENT TEXTS

INDEX OF SUBJECTS

INDEX OF AUTHORS